LADDERS *to* SUCCESS™

on the **State Assessment**

LEVEL **E**

PARENT-TEACHER COLLECTION

Reading

LEVELED INSTRUCTION AND PRACTICE ON
10 **ESSENTIAL SKILLS**

ACKNOWLEDGMENTS

"Rats May Be Used in Rescue Missions" contains quotations courtesy of http://www.newscientist.com

"Women's Stickball League Forms" contains quotations courtesy of http://www.palmbeachpost.com

"Teen Saves Life of Woman Who Saved His" contains quotations courtesy of http://www.wgrz.com

"Woman Invents Waterproof Paper" contains quotations courtesy of http://www.cleveland.com/plaindealer

"Beavers Use Stolen Money to Build Dam" contains quotations courtesy of The Associated Press

"New Jersey Governor Sinks Half-Court Shot" contains quotations courtesy of The Star-Ledger of Newark

"Bronx Students Win Robot Contests" contains quotations courtesy of http://www.columbia.edu/cu/news

"Philly Fears Snakehead Invasion" contains quotations courtesy of http://www.nationalgeographic.com

"Real-Life Batman Shares His Love of Bats" contains quotations courtesy of http://www.timeforkids.com

"Company Shut Down for Selling Land on Moon" contains quotations courtesy of http://www.chinadaily.com

"Students Relive Lewis and Clark's Journey" contains quotations courtesy of http://www.timeforkids.com and www.tri-cityherald.com

"Woman Sets Sailing Record" contains quotations courtesy of http://www.bbc.co.uk and http://www.scotsman.com

"Dinosaur Vomit Discovered" contains quotations courtesy of http://www.nationalgeographic.com

"Mayor Violates Snowball Law" contains quotations courtesy of http://www.usatoday.com

Page 11- A Hornbook, Corbis

Page 35-John Glenn, Corbis

Page 41-Kimani Ng'ang'a, Stan Honda/Getty Images

Page 55-Danny Way, Lucy Nicholson/Corbis

Page 69-Richard Codey, Jerry McCrea/Corbis

Page 76-Cheering Crowd, Frank Seguin/Corbis

Page 104-Aquarium of the Americas, Lowell Georgia/Corbis

Page 125-Ellen MacArthur, Reuters/Corbis

Ladders to Success, Reading Level E
179NA
ISBN-10: 1-59823-461-7
ISBN-13: 978-1-59823-461-9

Cover Image: Sam Ward/Mendola Artists

Triumph Learning® 136 Madison Avenue, 7th Floor, New York, NY 10016
Kevin McAliley, President and Chief Executive Officer

10 9 8 7

Table of Contents

Dear Student,

Welcome to **Ladders to Success** for Level E. This book will help you work on the ten reading skills most important to you this year. There is one lesson for each skill. You will master all ten skills by working through all ten lessons one by one.

This book does not rush you through a skill. Each lesson is fourteen pages long. This gives you plenty of time to really get comfortable learning what each skill means. You will see how each skill works in stories of different lengths.

The first page of every lesson is called Show What You Know. Take this short quiz to see how much you know about a skill before digging into the lesson. The next section, Guided Instruction 1, will start you off with some friendly guided review and practice. Practice the Skill 1, which follows Guided Instruction 1, shows you how to answer a multiple-choice question before asking you to try more by yourself. The next section, News Flash, is an exciting news story. It also comes with an activity.

Following the first News Flash is a three-page section called Ladder to Success. This section will give you three chances to practice the skill. Each practice is a little harder as you go "up the ladder." Now you are ready for the second part of the lesson.

The second part of the lesson is just like the first. You will see Guided Instruction 2, Practice the Skill 2, and another News Flash. This time around these sections are a little harder. The last 2 pages of each lesson are called Show What You Learned. Show off everything you learned in the lesson by correctly answering multiple-choice questions on the skill. Words that are boldfaced in the lessons appear in the glossary at the back of the book.

The lessons in this book will help you practice and improve your skills. They will also get you ready for the tests you will be taking this year. Some of the practice will be in the style of the state test. You will be answering multiple-choice and open-ended questions. You may see questions like these on your state test. Practicing with these types of questions will build your confidence.

We hope you will enjoy using *Ladders to Success.* We want you to climb the ladder to success this year. This book will help you get started!

Letter to the Family

Dear Parent or Family Member,

The **Ladders to Success** series of workbooks is designed to prepare your child to master ten of the fundamental skills in reading that are essential for success both in the curriculum and on state tests. *Ladders to Success* provides guided review and practice for the skills that are the building blocks of your child's education in reading. These are also the skills that will be tested on the state test in English Language Arts. Your child's success will be measured by how well he or she masters these skills.

Ladders to Success is a unique program in that each lesson is organized to ensure your child's success. Ten skills that students often find challenging are treated individually in ten lessons. Students are guided and supported through the first part of each lesson until they are ready to take on unguided practice in the second part of the lesson. Each lesson is fourteen pages long to give the student ample opportunity to review and practice a skill until a comfort level is reached. Support is gradually withdrawn throughout the lesson to build your student's confidence for independent work at the end of each lesson.

We invite you to be our partner in making learning a priority in your child's life. To help ensure success, we suggest that you review the lessons in this book with your child. You will see how each lesson gets subtly but progressively harder as you go along. While teachers will guide your child through the book in class, your support at home, added to the support of guided instruction and practice in the series, is vital to your child's comprehension.

We ask you to work with us this year to help your young student climb the ladder to success. Together, we can make a difference!

Letter to the Teacher

Dear Teacher,

Welcome to **Ladders to Success** in Reading for Level E. The Ladders to Success series of workbooks for reading is designed to prepare your students to master ten fundamental, grade-appropriate skills in reading that are essential for success both in the curriculum and on your state tests. Ladders provides guided review and practice for the skills that are the building blocks of the students' education. These are also skills that will be tested on your state tests in reading.

Ladders to Success is a unique program in that each lesson is leveled, or scaffolded, to ensure your students' success. Students are guided and supported through the first part of each lesson until they are ready to take on unguided practice in the second part of the lesson. Ten important skills are treated individually in ten lessons. Each lesson is fourteen pages long to give the student ample opportunity to review and practice a skill until a comfort level is reached. Support is slowly withdrawn throughout the lesson to build your students' confidence for independent work at the end of each lesson.

Ladders has a consistent, symmetrical format. The format is predictable from lesson to lesson, which increases students' comfort level with the presentation of skills-based information and practice. The first page of every lesson is called Show What You Know. This is a short diagnostic quiz to determine how much a student knows about a particular skill before digging into the lesson. It represents a snapshot of where each student is "now" before additional review and practice. This diagnostic quiz can be your guide in the way you choose to use the different parts of the lesson that follows.

The next section, Guided Instruction 1, will start students off slowly with guided review and practice. Practice the Skill 1, which immediately follows Guided Instruction 1, models how to answer a multiple-choice question before asking students to try more by themselves. The next section, News Flash, is an exciting contemporary news story that will engage students' interest. It is accompanied by an activity, often a graphic organizer, under the heading Write About It.

Following the first News Flash is a three-page section called Ladder to Success, which embodies the spirit of the Ladders series. This section provides three more chances to practice the skill. What makes this section unique is that each practice is a little harder as students go "up the ladder." By the time students have finished the third practice, they are ready for the second part of the lesson, which mirrors the first part. The Ladder to Success section is the crucial bridge between the first part of the lesson and the second.

Thus, you will now see Guided Instruction 2, Practice the Skill 2, and another News Flash. This time around, however, these sections are more challenging. The passages are longer and/or cognitively more difficult and there is less modeling. The activity under the Write About It heading in the second News Flash in each lesson, for example, is an unscaffolded writing activity.

The last two pages of each lesson represent a Posttest on the skill of the lesson. It is called Show What You Learned. Here is the student's chance to show off everything he or she learned in the lesson by successfully answering multiple-choice questions on the skill. The Posttest ends with an open-ended question, giving students the opportunity to show a deeper understanding of the skill now that they have completed the lesson. Words that are bold-faced in the lessons appear in the glossary at the back of the book.

Triumph Learning supports you in the difficult challenges you face in engaging your students in the learning process. *Ladders to Success* attempts to address some of these challenges by providing lessons that contain interesting material, scaffolded, or leveled, support, and a spectrum of multiple-choice questions and open-ended activities. This will allow students to build their confidence as they work towards proficiency with each skill in each lesson.

We ask you to work with us this year to help your students climb the ladder to success. Together, we *will* make a difference!

LADDERS
to SUCCESS

LESSON
1
Comparing and
Contrasting

Show What You Know

Before you begin this lesson, take this quiz to show what you know about comparing and contrasting. Read this story about a girl and her cousin. Then answer the questions.

Land vs. Water

My cousin Marco keeps telling me that I need to try surfing because I love skateboarding. He says the two sports have a lot in common. Both sports use boards, and you need a lot of balance to do tricks. He's right about that, but there is one thing that is *very* different. I ride my skateboard on land—he surfs in the ocean! Marco may enjoy swimming, but I don't like the water at all!

Another reason why Marco says that I'd like surfing is because it's fun to hang out at the beach after school with your friends. Of course I like to hang out with my friends. But unlike Marco, I go to the skate park, not the beach. All that sand is itchy!

I guess I should just give it a try. Marco and I both like sports. And we always have fun together. Maybe we aren't so different after all. We sure have one big thing in common when it comes to surfing and skateboarding – we both fall off our boards a lot!

Circle the letter of the best answer.

1. How are surfing and skateboarding alike?

   A They are both water sports.
   B They are both land sports.
   C They both use boards.
   D They both use parks.

2. According to the passage, both kids like to –

   A swim in the ocean
   B hang out with friends
   C play at the park
   D surf after school

3. How are the kids different?

   A One likes swimming.
   B One likes to have fun.
   C One likes sports.
   D One has a board.

4. What do the cousins have in common?

   A They both ride skateboards.
   B They both like the sand.
   C They both do difficult tricks.
   D They both fall off their boards a lot.

Introduction

When you **compare,** you find ways in which things are alike. When you **contrast,** you find ways in which things are different.

To compare and contrast,

- Look for words and phrases, such as *alike, also, too, same,* and *similarly* that signal comparisons.

- Look for words and phrases, such as *unlike, but, however, although,* and *on the other hand* that are clues to contrasts.

Here's How

Read this paragraph. Compare and contrast schools of today with schools of the 1700s.

School has changed a lot since the 1700s. Today, most students learn in big schools, but back in the 1700s, schools were small cabins.

Think About It

1. I see that the selection tells about schools today and schools of the 1700s.

2. One thing that is the same is that children go to school now, and they went to school in the 1700s. One thing that is different is that schools are big now, and they were small then.

3. The word *but* signals that the first part of the sentence will contrast schools today with those from long ago.

Try This Strategy

Scan and Skim

When you **scan and skim,** you look through a passage quickly to get an idea of what it is about or to find a particular part.

- Read the title and look at any pictures.
- Look for key words that help you focus on the ideas in the passage.
- Figure out whether the selection is fiction or nonfiction.

3 1833 05778 4388

Read this article. Use the Reading Guide for tips. The tips will help you scan and skim and compare and contrast as you read.

Reading Guide

Look for words that signal comparisons and contrasts.

Skim the text. Find differences and similarities in the details you read.

When do students go to school? How is this different from the way students went to school in the 1700s?

Going to School in the 1700s

School has changed a lot since the 1700s. Today, most students learn in big schools, but back in the 1700s, schools were small cabins. Instead of having a classroom and a teacher for each grade, all grades worked in one room with one teacher. Can you imagine sitting next to a first grader?

Students then were not as comfortable in class as kids are now. Students today have their own desks with chairs. Schools today are heated in the winter. Unlike students today, students in the 1700s sat on hard benches and had only a wood stove for warmth.

Like today, students in the 1700s learned to read in school. Instead of textbooks, children had **hornbooks** to help them learn. Hornbooks are wooden paddles covered with clear animal horn to protect them. Students today still cover their books. Some things never change!

Would you like to go to school only three months a year? It sounds great, but there was a catch. Like today, students in the 1700s stayed out of school for the summer. However, children in the 1700s worked on the family farms during that time. They only went to school in the winter. Maybe it sounds like fun to go to school less. But many kids back then never had the chance to finish school because they worked.

Now use what you learned to compare and contrast.

Answer the questions on the next page.

Practice the Skill 1

Practice comparing and contrasting in the article you just read.

EXAMPLE

One thing you have that children in the 1700s did not have is a —

A classroom

B chair

C school

D teacher

Think about the subject of the selection.

The article is about how schools in the 1700s were different from schools today.

What does the question ask?

This question asks about what I have that students of the past did not have. I know what schools have today. I need to figure out what students did not have in the past. The question asks about a difference between me and the students of long ago.

Look for signal words and phrases.

I see words that show contrast. The second paragraph tells what students had then, and what they have now. I see the word *unlike* and read that students had to sit on benches not chairs. The answer is *chairs*.

Now read each question. Circle the letter of the best answer.

1. One main difference between schools then and schools today is the —

    A subjects they teach

    B number of reading lessons

    C time of the year

    D comfort of classrooms

2. What word in the third paragraph signals a contrast?

    A still

    B help

    C Instead

    D never

3. What is similar about books then and now?

    A covered books

    B wood paddles

    C reading lessons

    D long chapters

4. Students now and students long ago both stay out of school in the —

    A spring

    B summer

    C fall

    D winter

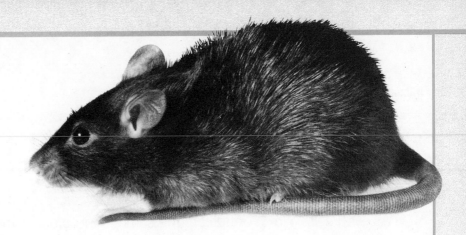

Rats May Be Used in Rescue Missions

Trained rats may take the place of dogs in rescue missions.

GAINESVILLE, FL—Move over, rescue dogs. A University of Florida study shows that rats may be better than dogs when it comes to finding earthquake survivors.

Like dogs, rats have a strong sense of smell. They also can **detect** human scents from under collapsed buildings. But because they are so small and quick, rats can crawl into tight spaces where dogs cannot. These rescue **rodents** could possibly find victims faster than dogs could. They could possibly help save more lives.

In a new study, scientists show how this could be done. The rats don't use movements to show where survivors are buried. Instead, the rats communicate with rescuers using only their brain waves. Each rat wears equipment that tracks its brain activity. As soon as a rat detects the human scent, its brain gives off a signal. The signal tells rescuers exactly where to start digging.

Rescue teams seem excited with the idea of using rats in their missions. "It would be absolutely fantastic," says rescue worker Julie Ryan. The rescue dog's job is safe for the moment, but perhaps not for much longer. Scientists hope to have a system using rats working soon.

Write About It

Now you will practice the skill using a real news story. Complete this graphic organizer. Compare and contrast details of what dogs and rats do to help rescue people.

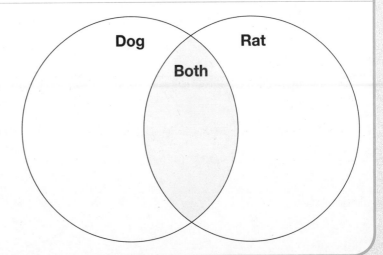

Dog   Rat

Both

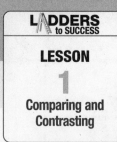
Review

You have learned to **compare and contrast** details from a story or article.

Review the steps you can use to compare and contrast.

- Ask yourself, "Which details are the same in this story? Which are different?"
- Look for words and phrases that signal comparison, such as *alike, also,* and *too.*
- Look for words and phrases that signal contrast, such as *unlike, but, however, otherwise,* and *on the other hand.*

Practice 1

Read the following story about twin brothers. As you read, think about what is the same about the brothers. Think about how they are different.

> "Yuck," said Todd, watching his twin make lunch. "I can't believe you put ketchup on a turkey-and-cheese sandwich. I like mustard."
>
> "I like mustard, too, but on salami. You shouldn't talk, anyway," Tom answered. "You put ice in your milk, and that's weird." The twins' mother interrupted, "At least you both like cookies. What kind do you want?"
>
> "Chocolate chip!" declared Todd.
>
> "But I want oatmeal raisin!" added Tom. Just then a delivery person arrived with a package. Seeing the boys, he exclaimed, "Wow, you are identical twins!"
>
> "Yes, we are exactly alike," answered Todd.

Use the Venn Diagram to compare and contrast the twins. Skim the passage to see the different things each boy likes. Then think of how they are the same.

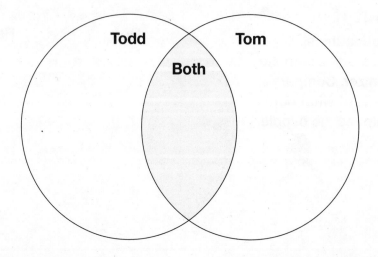

Practice 2

Read the passage. Think about how the book the librarian describes is similar to and different from the one the girl has read.

Jenny closed her book, frowning.

"Didn't you like your book?" Mr. Kim the librarian asked.

"*Harriet the Spy* was terrific, but that's the problem. I hate finishing a good book," Jenny explained. "I like how curious Harriet is and also that she lives in New York City, where I live. Plus, the book is **realistic** because a girl could spy on her friends and get into trouble when they found out. It was **hilarious**."

"Read *Harriet the Spy, Double Agent*," Mr. Kim suggested. "It's about the same character, but it is written by a different author. Sport is still her best friend, but Harriet meets someone new, Annie. They spy in their New York neighborhood, and their adventures are also really funny." Jenny checked out the book right away.

Use this graphic organizer to compare and contrast the two books in the story.

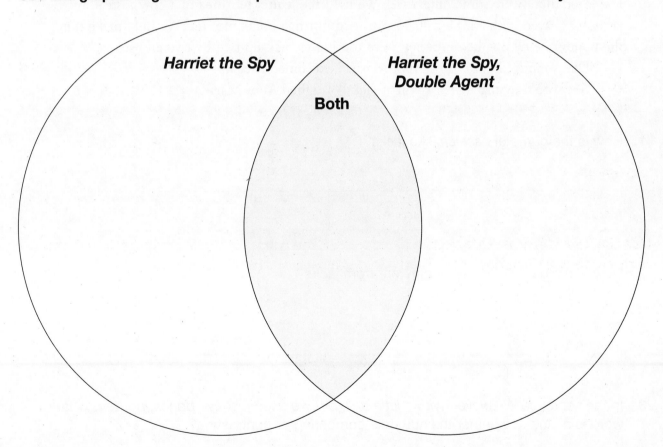

Practice 3

Read the passage. Then compare and contrast ideas in the story to answer the questions. Make a graphic organizer on a separate sheet of paper to organize your thoughts.

"Let's play jacks," Megan suggested to Aunt Marie.

"We didn't play that when I was a girl in Haiti, so I don't know how," Aunt Marie responded.

"I'll show you," Megan offered. She explained that each player drops ten jacks on the ground and tosses a little ball into the air. "Before the ball lands, you must pick up one jack," Megan demonstrated. She told Aunt Marie that the player repeats picking up one jack until all ten jacks have been picked up. Then she said, "The player starts again, this time picking up the jacks in twos, then in threes. The player keeps going until she has picked up all ten jacks at once. If you make a mistake picking up the jacks, the player's turn is over, and the next player tries."

"Oh, you should have said that jacks is like the game of *osselets*," Aunt Marie said smiling, but Megan looked confused. "We played a Haitian game that is similar to jacks. However, there were some differences. We used the **knucklebones** of a cow instead of jacks. We played with a little ball, but we used just five bones, not ten. We only picked up the bones one by one because they were too big to pick up two by two and so on."

"That sounds kind of gross, Aunt Marie!" exclaimed Megan.

"You won't say that when I win at jacks!" laughed Aunt Marie.

1. How is the game of *osselets* like jacks?

   _____

   _____

2. How is the game of *osselets* different from jacks?

   _____

   _____

3. In the sentence *We played with a little ball, but we used just five bones, not ten,* what word is a clue to whether the author is comparing or contrasting?

   _____

   _____

Introduction

As we read, we can **compare** things that are alike and **contrast** things that are different. **Comparing and contrasting** helps us understand, organize, and remember important details.

As you saw on pages 14–16, graphic organizers help you compare and contrast two subjects.

- In the top left box, write words and phrases that only describe the first subject.
- In the top right box, write words and phrases that only describe the second subject.
- In the bottom box, write descriptions that tell about both subjects.

Here's How

Read this paragraph about pandas. How are the two pandas alike and how are they different?

When someone mentions pandas, you probably think of the lovable-looking, large white animal with black markings. That is the *giant panda*, but it isn't the only kind of panda. There is another kind of panda called the *lesser* or *red panda*. This panda has reddish fur with white markings.

Think About It

Giant Pandas	Red Pandas
black and white	red and white
Both are pandas	

Try This Strategy

Visualize

When you visualize, you see pictures in your mind about what the author describes.

- As you read, look for describing words the author uses.
- Try to visualize the things the author describes by creating a picture in your mind. Think about what you might see, hear, feel, taste, and smell.

Read the article. Use the Reading Guide for tips that can help you visualize and compare and contrast as you read.

 Reading Guide

What kind of visual picture can you make in your mind about the pandas? Can you see how they are different?

What clue word lets you know that there is a difference in where the two kinds of pandas live?

What details in this paragraph tell how the pandas are similar? How do you know?

Pandas of a Different Color

When someone mentions pandas, you probably think of the lovable-looking, large white animal with black markings. That is the *giant panda*, but it isn't the only kind of panda. There is another kind of panda called the *lesser* or *red panda*. This panda has reddish fur with white markings. Both pandas may both look cuddly, but neither one makes a good pet.

Giant pandas live up to their name, growing about as tall as adult humans. They can weigh three hundred pounds, or about as much as two human adults. On the other hand, red pandas are only about two feet tall and weigh around eleven pounds.

Both giant and red pandas live in China, however red pandas are also found in India. Both pandas live in **bamboo** forests. The bamboo plant is a big part of the diet of both pandas. Both types of pandas use an extra thumb to hold their food. Giant pandas eat bamboo shoots, stems, and leaves. Similarly, red pandas prefer the bamboo leaves, but they also munch on grass, fruits, and berries.

All pandas are big eaters, spending over half the day looking for meals. Giant pandas eat 20–40 pounds of food a day. Red pandas eat half their weight in food per day and, like giant pandas, spend the rest of their time sleeping.

Answer the questions on the next page.

Practice the Skill 2

Practice comparing and contrasting by answering questions about the article you just read. Read each question. Circle the letter of the best answer.

1. Both giant and red pandas —

   A make good pets

   B have black fur

   C have extra thumbs

   D sit up to eat

2. Giant pandas are as tall as —

   A adult humans

   B lesser pandas

   C bamboo plants

   D red pandas

3. In the sentence *On the other hand, red pandas are only about two feet tall and weigh around eleven pounds*, the word or phrase that signals a contrast is —

   A about

   B weigh around

   C on the other hand

   D only

4. What is true about where giant and red pandas live?

   A Giant pandas and red pandas both live in China and India.

   B Giant pandas live in India, but red pandas do not.

   C Red pandas live in China, but giant pandas do not.

   D Red pandas live in India, but giant pandas do not.

5. Giant and red pandas both eat —

   A bamboo leaves

   B bamboo shoots

   C berries

   D grass

6. On a separate sheet of paper, write what is similar and different about the amounts of food that giant and red pandas eat.

Women's Stickball League Forms

Stickball is not just for children anymore.

PALM BEACH, FL—Women who never got a chance to play the neighborhood game of stickball as children are finally getting their chance. The Charlotte Russe Stickball League was recently formed in Palm Beach, Florida, and is mostly made up of women in their 50s or older.

Many of these women grew up in New York City watching the boys play stickball on the streets of their hometown. "We all have memories, even if we didn't play," says Marian Rosenberg, one of the league's three directors.

Stickball shares many of the same rules as baseball, but with a few major differences. Players use a stick, such as a mop or broom handle, to hit a ball. As in baseball, they also try to run the bases and score runs. Instead of a baseball field, though, teams often play right on the street, using manhole covers and parked cars as bases. The heavy baseball is also replaced with a pink rubber ball, or Spaldeen, so that surrounding windows don't break.

The Charlotte Russe League is one of the first stickball leagues that allows women to play. But given its popularity, it probably won't be the last. "It's been a lot of fun," says Rosenberg. "The girls that are doing it absolutely love it."

Write About It

Now you will practice the skill using a real news story. On a separate sheet of paper, describe how stickball and baseball are alike and how they are different.

Read this article about how kids around the world celebrate birthdays. Then answer the questions on the next page.

Happy Birthday to You!

How do you like to celebrate your birthday? Most kids in the United States think of a party with cake, presents, and the familiar "Happy Birthday" song. However, that picture probably isn't what kids in other parts of the world think of when it comes to a birthday celebration.

For instance, kids in Norway celebrate with a song, but not the way kids in the U.S. do. Norwegian kids celebrate at school. The birthday child picks a friend, and they dance in front of the class while everyone sings a special birthday song. Talk about being the center of attention!

Like in the United States, dessert plays an important role at a Russian birthday party. But don't look for a cake. Instead, Russian children find good wishes carved into birthday pie. In both countries kids are sure to get a piece of something sweet.

Similarly, Mexican kids celebrate with sweets, songs, and something very special – a piñata. A piñata is a hollow figure in the form of a star or other fun shape made of papier maché and filled with candy. Children take turns trying to break the piñata open with a stick. Then they rush to collect the candy that spills out. Mexico also has a special birthday song called "Las Mañanitas," or "Morning Verses."

Israeli children celebrate in a very different way at parties. The family decorates a special chair with flowers and plants. The birthday boy or girl sits in the chair, and everyone lifts him or her up one time for every year of his or her life plus one for good luck.

Some kids in eastern Canada also receive good-luck wishes on their birthday, although the tradition is quite unique. Family members chase the birthday boy or girl and rub his or her nose with butter or margarine when caught. The idea is to get his or her nose too slippery for bad luck to stick. That must get pretty messy! One thing must be the same with birthdays all around the world—it's all about the fun of celebrating!

Read each question. Circle the letter of the best answer.

1. Birthdays in the U.S. and Norway both have —

   A cake

   B songs

   C piñatas

   D butter

2. What word in the third paragraph signals a contrast?

   A like

   B important

   C instead

   D both

3. What makes Mexico's birthday celebration different from other countries?

   A songs

   B piñatas

   C cake

   D flowers

4. According to the passage, which countries celebrate with birthday songs?

   A Mexico and Norway

   B Israel and Norway

   C Mexico and Canada

   D Israel and Canada

5. According to the passage, one way all the celebrations described are alike is that in each country, —

   A children eat sweets

   B a song is sung

   C children celebrate at school

   D having fun is the most important thing

6. The article does not mention sweets or desserts being eaten to celebrate birthdays in —

   A Israel

   B Mexico

   C United States

   D Russia

7. What do celebrations in Canada and Israel have in common?

   A good-luck wishes

   B flowers and plants

   C sweets and desserts

   D chairs to lift people on

8. On a separate sheet of paper, tell which country's birthday celebrations are most like the United States' and which are most different. Support your answer with details from the article. ✎

Show What You Know

Before you begin this lesson, take this quiz to show what you know about sequence. First, read this story about making a snowman. Then answer the questions that follow.

Snowman Day

Leisha loves snow days. When she wakes up and sees flakes coming down furiously, she knows there won't be any school. It isn't just a snow day to her—it's a *snowman* day.

Making a snowman is one of Leisha's favorite things to do on a snowy day. It's a good thing she lives in snowy Chicago! The first thing she does is test the snow quality. It needs to be wet and heavy. Then she **enlists** the help of her sister to roll out three big snowballs in the backyard. The third thing they have to do is stack the balls to make the snowman's body. Then they find sticks for arms. Sometimes they take a break to warm up and have a hot chocolate.

After the break, Leisha heads back out to give the snowman a real personality. One of her favorite creations was a snowman dressed in old swim trunks and a sun hat, holding a bottle of sunscreen. Her neighbors thought that was pretty funny since it was only 20 degrees outside! The last thing that Leisha does is write her signature in the snow at the base of the snowman. She likes to take credit for her work.

Circle the letter of the best answer.

1. What does Leisha do first when she makes a snowman?

   A finds her sister

   B wakes up

   C tests the snow

   D drinks hot chocolate

2. What happens after Leisha and her sister roll snowballs?

   A They stack the snowballs.

   B They look for sticks.

   C They dress the snowman.

   D They warm up inside.

3. When does Leisha give the snowman a personality?

   A before they roll snowballs

   B after they find sticks

   C before it snows

   D after the break

4. What is Leisha's last step?

   A drinking hot chocolate

   B writing her signature

   C looking for clothes

   D talking to her neighbors

Introduction

Sequence is the order in which things happen. When we use sequence, we put things in the order in which they happened. We tell what happened first, next, and last.

To put things in sequence,

- Think about the events that happen in the passage.
- Think about the order of those events. Which happened first? Next? Last?
- Clue words can help you follow the order of events. Some clue words are *first, next, last, then, before,* and *after*. Also pay attention to dates, time words, and phrases, such as *next week, in a month,* and *a year later.*

Here's How

Read this paragraph. Look at the events to understand the sequence.

Then it's time to find our seats. Before sitting down, we have to put on our baseball gloves. Finally, Jason takes out his score sheet and a pencil.

Think About It

1. The people in the story are getting ready for a game to start.

2. I can tell by reading that they find their seats, put on their gloves, sit, and take out the score sheets and a pencil.

3. I know the order because I notice the words *then, before,* and *finally.*

Try This Strategy

Access Prior Knowledge

Before reading a passage, look at the title and the pictures to see what the passage is about. Then think of what you already know about the topic. Think about what you would like to learn.

- Look at the title and the pictures. Decide what the passage is about.
- Ask yourself what you already know about the subject.
- Think about personal experiences you have had, books you have read, or movies you have seen that have something to do with the topic.

Read the story. Use the Reading Guide for tips. The tips can help you access prior knowledge and understand sequence as you read.

Reading Guide

Decide what the topic of the story is. What do you know about going to the ballpark?

Think about what happens first in the story.

Figure out what happens next. Several things happen at one time.

Look for events that happen last.

A Winning Routine at the Ballpark

I like going to the ballpark with my friend Jason because he is so **superstitious.** He follows the same routine for every game to make sure our team wins.

First, we have to enter the park at door number one and go to the third **turnstile,** where Old Joe is always tearing tickets. Jason always asks, "Joe, are we going to win today?" Joe always answers, "Sure thing!"

The next step is to buy a hot dog and a soda. We can't order anything else. If I want a pretzel, Jason looks at me sternly and says, "We don't have pretzels until the seventh inning!"

Then it's time to find our seats. Before sitting down, we have to put on our baseball gloves. Finally, Jason takes out his score sheet and a pencil. He is always ready just in time for the first pitch.

During the game we have to clap when there's a hit and stand up for any runs. We have a great time. Sometimes we even win. At the end, Jason likes to sit and watch the people leave. I don't mind waiting, but I'd like to have an ice cream, just to see what happens.

Now use what you learned about sequence.

Answer the questions on the next page.

Practice understanding the sequence of events in the story you just read.

EXAMPLE

When does Jason sit down?

A   before buying a hot dog
B   after the first pitch
C   during the seventh inning
D   after putting on his glove

Think about the events that happen in the passage.

I know that Jason does things in order at the ballpark. I need to remember all the steps.

Think about the order of those events. Which happened first? Next? Last?

First Jason buys a hot dog. Next he puts on his glove. Then he sits down. The first pitch comes next, and the seventh inning is later in the game.

Look for clue words such as first, next, then, before, and after.

I see the word before, and I know the word is a clue about when Jason sits down.

Now read each question. Circle the letter of the best answer.

1. What happens first?

   A   They buy a pretzel.
   B   They talk to Joe.
   C   They get a hot dog and a soda.
   D   They enter at door number one.

2. After buying hot dogs, the two friends —

   A   go through the turnstile
   B   watch the first pitch
   C   find their seats
   D   watch the people leave

3. What happens before the first pitch?

   A   Jason takes out his score sheet.
   B   Jason eats a pretzel.
   C   Jason stands up for a run.
   D   Jason claps for a hit.

4. What happens at the end of the game?

   A   They eat a pretzel.
   B   They watch people leave.
   C   They win the game.
   D   They buy ice cream.

NEWS FLASH!

Teen Saves Life of Woman Who Saved His

Kevin Stephan gave Penny Brown flowers after saving her life.

BUFFALO, NY—In an odd **coincidence,** a western New York teen saved the life of a woman who saved his life years earlier.

In 1999, eleven-year-old Kevin Stephan was a bat boy for his younger brother's baseball team. Kevin was hit in the chest by a baseball bat when the bat slipped out of a player's hands. He stopped breathing. Luckily, Penny Brown was there. Penny, a nurse whose son played on that team, gave Kevin CPR. She brought the young boy back to life.

Almost seven years later, Kevin Stephan returned the favor. In a twist of fate, Penny and Kevin both happened to be at the same restaurant. When Penny Brown began choking on her food, Kevin quickly gave Penny the Heimlich maneuver until she coughed up her food. Shortly after, they realized the coincidence. Penny and Kevin were both pretty amazed. "It's almost unbelievable," said Kevin, who is now seventeen years old.

The two met again a few days later. This time, however, no one's life was in danger. Kevin gave Penny a bouquet of flowers.

Write About It

In the chart below, write four events that were described in this article. Write them in time order.

1.	2.	3.	4.

Ladder to Success

Review

As you read, you can use clues to help you to **understand the sequence** of events. These clues will help you keep track of the order in which things happen.

Review the steps you can use to understand sequence.

- Think about the events that happen in the passage.
- Think about what happened first, next, and last.
- Look for clue words, such as *then, before,* and *after*. Notice time words and phrases, such as *next week, in a month,* and *a year later.*

Practice 1

Read the following article about how fireflies develop. Think about the life stages the insects go through.

You see fireflies flashing their lights on June nights. Like all insects, fireflies follow stages in the life cycle. First, female fireflies lay eggs on wet soil. The eggs hatch into wormlike larvae, which give off light. People call them glowworms. Glowworms eat snails, earthworms, and the larvae of other insects, all of which help them grow. A year or two later, the glowworms enter the pupa stage, during which they finally change into an adult insect. Finally, adult fireflies produce eggs, and the cycle starts again.

Use the life cycle chart below to show the life stages of a firefly.

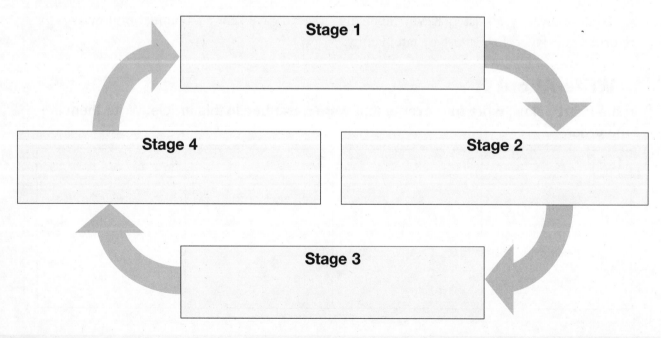

Practice 2

Read the passage. What was the sequence of events in the life of toy trains?

Toy trains have been a favorite plaything since the 1500s. The first toy trains were called floor-runners. They were made of tin or wood, and they had a long string attached that children pulled. In the 1600s, the floor-runners were improved. By the 1700s, the floor-runners were replaced by windup toys. Then a hundred years later, steam-powered toy trains were invented.

Around 1900, a teen named Joshua Lionel Cohen had a great idea. He made a toy train that ran on electricity. He thought it would be great to sell his train so other kids could play with trains too. A local store put one in the window. Soon people were buying the electric toy trains faster than the boy could make them. Josh started the Lionel train company, which still exists today.

Use this graphic organizer to show how toy trains changed over time.

Toy Trains	
1500s	
1600s	
1700s	
1800s	
1900s	

Practice 3

Read the passage. Then answer the questions about the sequence of events. Make a graphic organizer on a separate sheet of paper to organize your thoughts.

> Birds flocked to Grandma's feeder to feast on seeds. However, so did a pesky squirrel. Grandma really wanted to get rid of that squirrel. First, she tried putting the bird feeder on a pole, but her friendly squirrel was an expert pole climber. A few weeks later, she decided to hang the feeder from a rope, but the clever squirrel was also a trapeze artist.
>
> After that, Grandma thought if she changed the food, the squirrel might go away. This squirrel was not a picky eater, and he gobbled up whatever was served. Grandma's next brainstorm was to hang a wind chime from the feeder. She hoped the noise would scare away the squirrel. Sadly, it scared away the birds, too.
>
> At last, Grandma thought of the old saying, "If you can't beat 'em, join 'em." She decided to give up and make a "dining room" just for the squirrel. She built a squirrel feeder and put it far from the bird feeder. This made the squirrel very happy. He had never liked sharing meals with those noisy, chirping birds anyway. Now, Grandma only had one problem. How was she going to keep the birds out of the squirrel feeder?

1. What was Grandma's first plan?

_____

_____

2. What did Grandma do just before she put the wind chime near the feeder?

_____

_____

3. What three sequence words or phrases were used in the story?

_____

_____

Introduction

When you read, the **sequence** of events is not always clear right away. Thinking about what happened first, next, and last will help you understand and put events in order.

As you saw on pages 27–29, graphic organizers help you understand sequence.

- In each box, write something that happens in the passage.
- Look for clue words to help you decide what order to write the events in.

Here's How

Read this paragraph. What does Dad do first?

First, he takes out at least two boxes of cereal. Then he combines the cereals in a bowl. Next, he thinly slices strawberries and bananas.

Think About It

Step 1:
Chooses cereal boxes

Step 2:
Combines cereals

Step 3:
Slices strawberries and bananas

Try This Strategy

Summarize

Here's another strategy to help you understand sequence. When you **summarize,** you retell the most important parts of a story or passage in your own words.

- As you read, keep track of the most important parts or events.
- When you finish reading, try to restate the most important parts in your own words.
- Reread the passage, and think about what happened at the beginning, in the middle, and at the end.

Read the story. Use the Reading Guide for tips to help you summarize and understand the sequence of events as you read.

 Reading Guide

What is Dad making? Watch for steps that show sequence.

What kinds of clue words tell you the sequence of events?

Summarize the passage. How could you describe Dad's process in your own words?

A Perfect Bowl of Cereal

My dad believes there is an art to eating cereal. I think it's weird, but he thinks the ordinary things in life are beautiful. *Whatever.*

His first concern is his tools. He must have a deep cereal bowl, a small spoon, and a sharp knife. "The tools of the trade," he likes to say. What trade is that, Dad? Professional cereal engineer?

Next, he turns to his ingredients. Dad wouldn't think of only using one kind of cereal. Oh no, not my dad. First, he takes out at least two boxes of cereal and combines them in a bowl. Next, he thinly slices strawberries and bananas. Otherwise, he could scoop up a big chunk of fruit with no cereal. What a catastrophe!

Then the weirdness continues. Normal people put the cereal in the bowl and then drop the fruit on top. My dad gets out another bowl. Then he layers the cereal with the fruit so that the fruit is "evenly **distributed.**"

The final step is the milk, which Dad keeps in the refrigerator until the last minute so it will be ice cold. (The process takes a while, as you can imagine.) He pours the milk just to the level of the cereal for proper liquid **absorption.**

Only then does he eat. I guess I can live with his "masterpiece" because it makes him really happy.

Answer the questions on the next page.

Practice understanding sequence by answering questions about the story you just read. Read each question. Circle the letter of the best answer.

1. What does Dad gather when he begins?

   A milk

   B cereal

   C fruit

   D tools

2. Dad slices the fruit after —

   A combining the cereals

   B layering the fruit

   C pouring the milk

   D taking a bite

3. What is the first thing that goes into a bowl?

   A cereal

   B nuts

   C fruit

   D milk

4. What does Dad do after he pours the milk?

   A finds a spoon

   B eats the cereal

   C gets out another bowl

   D slices the fruit

5. At the very last minute Dad —

   A eats the cereal

   B layers the fruit

   C pours the milk

   D mixes the cereal

6. On a separate sheet of paper, write Dad's way of preparing cereal as a recipe with steps in the correct order.

Woman Invents Waterproof Paper

Sally Ramsey invented paper that is waterproof.

AKRON, OH—Writing will never be the same again. Ohio chemist Sally Ramsey has invented a new form of waterproof paper. And she did it completely by accident.

In June of 2005, Ramsey was working in her chemical lab in Akron doing tests on a new chemical spray. She was about to throw away a piece of paper used to protect her equipment from the spray, when she got an idea. After exposing the paper to UV light to let it dry, Ramsey tried writing on it with a pen. To her surprise, her writing showed up clearly.

When she dipped the paper in water, she discovered that the writing did not smudge or fade like it would with regular paper. She was even able to write on it again after taking the paper out of the water.

Ramsey's accidental invention could have a number of uses. She is already talking to companies to use the chemical on everything from address labels to sports equipment.

When asked about this exciting invention, Ramsey shrugged it off as just one of 12 different chemicals she has invented. "This one's just the most fun, I guess." Talk about being modest!

Write About It

On a separate sheet of paper, describe how Sally Ramsey invented waterproof paper. Include at least three events and the order in which they occurred.

Read this article about John Glenn. Then answer the questions on the next page.

John Glenn: AMERICAN HERO

Can you imagine flying at 18,000 miles per hour? That's equal to covering five miles in one second! John Glenn traveled that speed when he became the first American to orbit the earth in 1962.

John Herschel Glenn, Jr. always had a passion for flying. Born on July 18, 1921 in Cambridge, Ohio, John was eight years old when he took his first plane ride. In 1938, he traveled to the Cleveland National Air Races with his father. There, they watched aircraft contests and stunts. Three years later, John took flying lessons and earned his pilot's license.

A few years after, John became a fighter pilot in World War II. He also fought in the Korean War. John was a leader and won many medals for his excellent flying skills.

In 1958, NASA was established. John was chosen to be one of the first seven astronauts in space. President Eisenhower selected the men. He said that John was sensible and a good decision maker. John also received the highest scores on NASA's physical and mental tests. After ten delays, the *Friendship 7* spacecraft finally took off in 1962. As the third American in space, John circled the earth three times. John Glenn became a hero for **manually** operating the spacecraft when part of it seemed to **malfunction.**

After that adventure, John became involved in politics. He was elected to the United States Senate in 1974. He was well liked by many people. He was hard working, very smart, and a problem solver. In 1983, he decided to run for U.S. president. One year later, he had a serious fall and was so seriously injured that he pulled out of the race.

In 1998, thirty-six years after his first flight, NASA sent John on another space challenge. He boarded the *Space Shuttle Discovery* for a nine-day mission to see how weightlessness affects the body of an older person. This time, John circled the earth 134 times and, at 77 years old, he became the oldest person ever to go into space.

John Glenn has all the qualities of an American hero.

Read each question. Circle the letter of the best answer.

1. What happened one year after John Glenn decided to run for president?

   A He earned his pilot's license.

   B He had a serious fall.

   C He became a fighter pilot.

   D He boarded the *Space Shuttle Discovery* for a nine-day mission.

2. John Glenn's first space mission was in —

   A 1958

   B 1921

   C 1998

   D 1962

3. What did John do three years before he earned his pilot's license?

   A He attended the Cleveland National Air Races with his father.

   B He took his first plane ride.

   C He became a fighter pilot.

   D He fought in the Korean War.

4. The article states that John became involved in politics —

   A after his flight on board the *Space Shuttle Discovery*

   B before he became involved in the Korean War

   C before he was part of NASA

   D after his flight on board the *Friendship 7*

5. Which of these events was John Glenn's first flying experience?

   A He became a fighter pilot.

   B He flew the *Friendship 7.*

   C He took flying lessons.

   D He became the oldest person ever to go into space.

6. John Glenn was a fighter pilot —

   A during World War II

   B while he was an astronaut

   C after he ran for president

   D before he earned his pilot's license

7. What was John Glenn's last flying adventure?

   A flying in World War II

   B flying at the air races

   C flying on the shuttle *Discovery*

   D flying on *Friendship 7*

8. On a separate sheet of paper, create a timeline that shows the major events in John Glenn's life. Put the events in order, with the date underneath the line and the event above the line. Include at least five events on your timeline.

Show What You Know

Before you begin this lesson, take this quiz to show what you know about cause and effect. Read this story about a special cake. Then answer the questions.

Lake Cake

Ryan spent all day making a cake for Uncle Dan. He planned an **elaborate** lake scene for the top of the cake. He used green frosting for the canoe. He placed a toy soldier in the canoe to be Uncle Dan because he couldn't make a man out of frosting.

Since it was really hot outside, Ryan knew the cake needed to be kept cold. That was going to be a problem because the refrigerator was full. Then his brother Henry walked into the kitchen.

"What's that?" he asked.

"SHHH!" Ryan replied. "It's a surprise for Uncle Dan!"

"Look out! He's coming in right now!"

Ryan tried frantically to shove the cake into the refrigerator with both hands, but the cake was too big. He took a step back and bumped into Uncle Dan, who was just walking in. The cake went flying into the air and landed on the floor with a thud.

"What's the **commotion** all about, guys?" asked Uncle Dan.

"At least it landed facing up," Henry said laughing.

Uncle Dan said, "I love it! I've always a wanted to go over a waterfall in my canoe."

Circle the letter of the best answer.

1. Why did Ryan use a toy soldier on the cake?

   A because it was hot outside

   B because the canoe was green

   C because frosting wouldn't work

   D because Henry told him to

2. Ryan had to put the cake in a cold place because —

   A Uncle Dan came in

   B it was hot outside

   C the freezer was full

   D the cake was big

3. Why did the cake fall?

   A Ryan bumped into Uncle Dan.

   B Henry distracted Ryan.

   C The cake was too big to hold.

   D Henry came into the kitchen.

4. The kitchen scene caused Uncle Dan to feel —

   A mad

   B curious

   C uncomfortable

   D sad

A **cause** is an event that makes something happen. The **effect** is what happens.

To recognize cause and effect,

- Read and look for details that tell what happened.
- Think about each event. Ask yourself, "Why did this happen?"
- Look for clue words, such as *so, therefore,* and *as a result* to find the effect. Look for clue words such as *because* and *since* to find the cause.

Here's How

Read this paragraph. Look for what caused the ball to bounce away.

Jen watched the opposing players pass the ball up the court. The center passed to the point guard, but she missed it. As a result, the ball bounced away.

Think About It

1. I look for *details* to tell me what happens. I *see* that the ball bounced away.

2. Then I think about *why* the ball bounced away, and I *see* that the point guard missed the ball.

3. I read the phrase *as a result*. I know that this means that the ball bounced away because the point guard missed it.

Monitor and Clarify

When you **monitor and clarify,** you check to make sure you understand what you are reading.

- After reading each section, pause and try to restate the main ideas.
- If you did not understand the main ideas, reread the section. As you reread each sentence, restate the ideas in your own words.

Read the passage. Use the Reading Guide for tips. The tips will help you monitor and clarify and recognize cause and effect as you read.

Reading Guide

Check to make sure you understand the section. Tell about the game in your own words. Reread if you need help.

Look for details to understand the events and why they happen.

The word so *signals an effect. Look for the action and see why it happens.*

FULL-COURT SHOT

There was no way to win the basketball game. The visiting team, the Bulldogs, had hit a three-point shot, so they were one point ahead. Only six seconds remained in the game. The Bulldogs dribbled the ball slowly, hoping the clock would run out. They weren't going to give the Knights a chance to score if they could help it.

Jen watched the opposing players pass the ball up the court. The center passed to the point guard, but she missed it. As a result, the ball bounced away. So Jen got her chance.

Jen darted forward and grabbed the ball with only one second left. She threw the ball one-handed, launching it across the court since they were out of time. The buzzer sounded. She turned and began to walk away. There was no way that shot would make it.

Suddenly, the crowd roared, so Jen turned back and saw the ball falling through the net to the ground beneath it. She'd made the basket! The Knights won the game because of her one crazy shot.

Now use what you learned to recognize cause and effect.

Answer the questions on the next page.

Practice the Skill 1

Practice recognizing cause and effect in the story you just read.

EXAMPLE	Look for the event in the text.
What caused Jen to turn back at the end?	I reread and find that Jen turns back in the last paragraph.
A the sound of the ball in the net	**Look for signal words near the event.**
B the sound of the crowd roaring	I see the word *so*, which tells me that Jen's turning back is an effect.
C the sound of the buzzer	**Look for the event that makes this effect happen.**
D the sound of the ball bouncing	The crowd roars and that is what causes Jen to turn back.

Now read each question. Circle the letter of the best answer.

1. The Bulldogs were ahead because —

   A they watched the clock
   B they passed to the center
   C they dribbled the ball slowly
   D they hit a three-point shot

2. When did Jen grab the ball?

   A when the ball bounced away
   B when the clock ran out
   C when the buzzer sounded
   D when they hit a three-point shot

3. Why did Jen have to launch the ball across the court?

   A The Knights were one point ahead.
   B They were out of time.
   C The center passed the ball.
   D The game was over.

4. Why did the Knights win?

   A Jen made a crazy shot.
   B The clock ran out.
   C Jen passed the ball.
   D The buzzer sounded.

85-YEAR-OLD BEGINS SCHOOL

Kimani is over 70 years older than his classmates.

NEW YORK, NY—A Kenyan man is proving that it's never too late to learn. Eighty-five-year-old Kimani Ng'ang'a is attending primary school for the first time in his life. He is the world's oldest pupil.

As a young boy, Kimani never went to school because his family couldn't afford the Kenyan government's school fees. Eight decades later, he was finally able to begin his education when the Kenyan government dropped the fees. Kimani is helping to bring attention to the many children worldwide who cannot afford to attend school. He does not want them to wait as long as he did. The Kenyan student recently took time out of his busy school schedule to spread his message in New York.

Kimani, who uses two hearing aids and walks with a cane, is a straight-A student. He is focusing his studies on math, science, English, and his native language, Swahili. A father of 15, Kimani has grandchildren several grades ahead of him in school!

Write About It

Now practice the skill using a real news story. Complete this graphic organizer by filling in the cause that led to the effect.

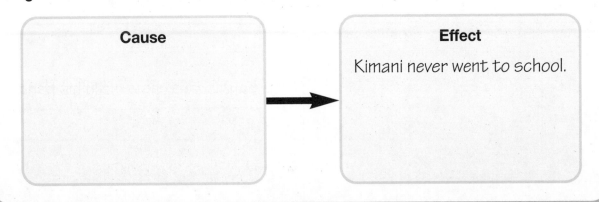

Cause	Effect
	Kimani never went to school.

Review

You have learned how to **recognize cause and effect**. A **cause** is an event that makes something happen. The **effect** is what happens.

Review the steps to recognize cause and effect.

- Read to find details about events in the story.
- Think about each event. Ask yourself, "Why did this happen?"
- Look for clue words, such as *so, therefore, as a result, because,* and *since.*

Practice 1

Read the following passage. As you read, think about the events. Ask yourself why each event happened. Look for clue words to help you find the cause and effect.

> Chris and Dan had taken the bicycle apart, cleaned it, and put it back together. As they admired their work, Chris noticed a bolt on the ground.
> "Where did this come from?" he asked, picking it up.
> "Maybe someone dropped it," Dan said. It looked like it had come from the bicycle. Dan decided to test the bike, so he rode it down the ramp. As he reached the bottom of the ramp, the handlebars came off in his hands because something was missing.
> "Uh-oh," Dan said. He jumped off the bike, which toppled over against a garbage can.
> "You might want that bolt," Chris said, holding it out in his palm.

Use the chart below to identify cause and effect. Ask yourself why the event happened. Write why the event happened under Cause.

Cause	Effect
	The handlebars came off in his hands.

Practice 2

Read the passage. What were the effects of the rain on the party?

When the rain began, Jasper had just started opening presents. Everyone let out a groan. The ice cream melted into puddles, and the ribbons and wrapping paper on his presents turned wet and mushy.

Jasper stood still, looking up at the clouds. Thanks to the rain, he thought, no one was going to have fun at his party. They would go to school and tell everyone what a bad time they'd had at Jasper's.

One girl, Shiree, was also standing in the rain, but she wasn't frowning. She loved the rain, so she held out her hands and smiled.

"Isn't it great?" she shouted. Soon, people began coming outside and standing with her.

"Come on, Jasper!" she said, twirling. Jasper looked around. Everyone at the party was outside again, enjoying the rain.

Use this graphic organizer to recognize cause and effect.

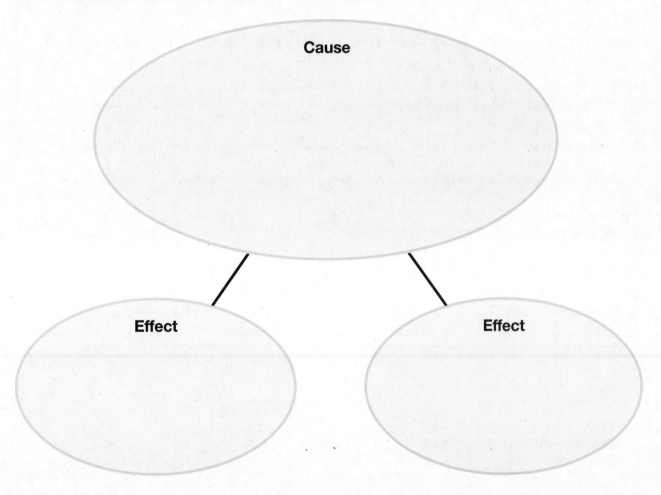

Practice 3

Read the passage. Then answer the questions by recognizing cause and effect. On a separate sheet of paper, make a graphic organizer to organize your thoughts.

> Leah wasn't in the mood to show the new girl around.
>
> "Your name's Tasha?" she asked. The girl nodded. She was dressed up, wearing a skirt and a button-down blouse. Everyone else wore jeans and sweatshirts. Leah was going to make a joke, but she decided against it because she knew how Tasha felt. Leah had felt like an outsider before, too.
>
> "Here's the gym. Do you play sports?" Leah asked. Tasha shook her head. Leah led Tasha through the cafeteria. The girl never said a word. They came back in near the music room.
>
> "We have a jazz band. Do you play an instrument?" Leah asked.
>
> "I play drums," Tasha said. Leah couldn't imagine this girl banging on the drums, since she was so quiet.
>
> "Huh," she said. "I sing." Tasha nodded.
>
> The next day, Leah was hanging out with her friends when Tasha walked up to them. Tasha handed Leah a CD that said "Tasha's Beats."
>
> "Maybe you can sing over them," Tasha said before disappearing. Leah looked at the album cover, which showed Tasha sitting at a drum set in her button-down blouse. Seeing her like that caused Leah to see Tasha in a new light.
>
> "Who's that?" asked one of Leah's friends.
>
> "A friend," said Leah.

1. What made Leah decide not to say anything about Tasha's clothes?

_____

_____

2. What was it about Tasha that caused Leah to be surprised that she played drums?

_____

_____

3. What caused Leah's opinion of Tasha to change?

_____

_____

Introduction

To **recognize cause and effect,** you look for events and why they happen. A **cause** makes something happen, and the **effect** is what happens as a result of the cause.

As you saw on pages 41–43, graphic organizers can help you recognize cause and effect.

- In the first box, write the cause that makes something happen.
- In the second box, explain what happens as a result.

Here's How

Read these sentences. What causes the Mohawks to be admired?

On the job, the young men worked with balance and strength at high altitudes above the swiftly moving river. They were admired for their bravery because they worked at those heights as if they were walking confidently down a forest path.

Think About It

Cause	Effect
The young men worked high in the air with confidence.	The young men were admired for their bravery.

Try This Strategy

Visualize

Here's another strategy to help you recognize cause and effect. When you **visualize,** you use details from what you read to form a picture in your mind.

- As you read, pay attention to how the writer describes the events taking place.
- Use those details to form a mental picture of the events you are reading about.
- Imagine the events like a movie taking place in front of you.

Read the article. Use the Reading Guide for tips to help you visualize and recognize cause and effect as you read.

Reading Guide

Look for details about cause and effect. Why were the workers called Skywalkers?

Look for clue words. What is the effect of the Mohawks letting the railroad use the land?

Imagine working on the bridge. What details help you visualize the event?

Why did many Mohawks relocate for these jobs?

Skywalkers

Many of the most famous landmarks in New York City were built with the help of the Native American Mohawk tribe. These courageous **laborers** are called *Skywalkers* because of their talent for working hundreds of feet in the air without showing any fear. This proud tradition began over 100 years ago.

In 1886, a Canadian railroad company wanted to build a bridge over the St. Lawrence River. The Mohawks agreed to allow the use of their lands since the company offered to give them jobs.

On the job, the young men worked with balance and strength at high altitudes above the swiftly moving river. They were admired for their bravery because they worked at those heights as if they were walking confidently down a forest path. The Mohawks quickly gained a **reputation** for being fearless when working at great heights. As a result they started working on skyscrapers in the United States.

Many Mohawk men relocated hundreds of miles for high-paying jobs working on buildings in New York City. The working conditions were treacherous and, as a result, the jobs paid high wages. The Skywalkers helped construct the Empire State Building and the Waldorf Astoria Hotel. Their descendants are still working these high-flying jobs today.

Answer the questions on the next page.

Practice the Skill 2

Practice recognizing cause and effect by answering questions about the article you just read. Read each question. Circle the letter of the best answer.

1. Why were the Mohawk workers called *Skywalkers*?

   A They walked on forest paths.

   B They worked in New York City.

   C They worked at great heights without fear.

   D They were paid high wages for taking risks.

2. The Mohawks agreed to let the railroad company use their land when —

   A the bridge was almost finished

   B they had a good reputation

   C the company went to New York

   D the company offered them jobs

3. Why were the Mohawk workers admired?

   A They were brave on the job.

   B They relocated hundreds of miles.

   C They built the Empire State Building.

   D They still work today.

4. Why were the Mohawks working on buildings in the United States?

   A They liked building skyscrapers.

   B They had a reputation for being fearless.

   C They accepted low pay.

   D They wanted to relocate in New York City.

5. How did the conditions of the job affect the wages that the Mohawk men received?

   A The conditions made the wages high.

   B The conditions made the wages low.

   C The conditions made the wages late.

   D The conditions made the wages hard to earn.

6. On a separate sheet of paper, write about how the Skywalkers' bravery helped build famous skyscrapers.

The beavers used sticks, mud, and money to build their dam.

Beavers Use Stolen Money to Build Dam

GREENSBURG, LA—Leave it to beavers to find a new use for money. Several bags of money stolen from a Louisiana casino turned up, of all places, in a beaver creek. The beavers discovered the money, so they put it to good use by weaving it into their dams. Saint Helena Parish deputies knew to search the creek when the thief's lawyer, hoping to strike a deal, told them the location of the three bags of money.

Deputies spotted the first two bags quickly but had trouble finding the last bag. That's when they came across the beaver dam and its expensive walls. Police took the dam apart piece-by-piece to recover the thousands of dollars weaved into the walls. Apparently, the beavers were careful with their money. "They hadn't torn the bills up. [The bills] were still whole," said Major Michael Martin, one of the officers on the scene.

In all, deputies found about $40,000 of the $70,000 stolen from the casino in the beaver dam.

Write About It

Reread this sentence from the article: "Leave it to beavers to find a new use for money." On a separate sheet of paper, explain what events led to the beavers using the money.

Read this article about wastewater treatment. Then answer the questions on the next page.

DOWN THE DRAIN

You get up in the morning, use the toilet, take a shower, and brush your teeth. Where does all that water go when it runs down the drain? You probably know that it flows into the **sewer.** But where does sewer water go? We don't just dump sewer water into rivers and oceans since that would pollute the plants, animals, and people near that water. In addition, imagine the smell!

People once threw their wastewater, or sewer water, right into rivers, or even into the street. Today, the wastewater travels to wastewater treatment plants, where it is cleaned and processed so that it is safe to return to nature.

Pipes in your home carry the water into a large sewer pipe. Other buildings, such as businesses and factories, also release dirty water into the sewers. All the sewer pipes in a city or town lead to a wastewater treatment plant. The water passes through a screen so that any large solid objects, such as pieces of wood or plastic bottles, can be taken out and thrown away. Then the water goes through a series of tanks. **Bacteria** in these tanks begin to break down the food scraps, soaps, and paper floating in the water. They break down these solids into stinky gases. Then, the water is shaken with a lot of air because the air helps the bacteria work. The air also helps to get rid of that smell!

Then the water is sent to another set of tanks, where it lies still. All the solid parts settle to the bottom, and any oily scum rises to the top. The scum is scraped off, and the solid material is hauled away. The water passes through a final filter, such as sand. As a result of the filtering, the water is free of most of the bacteria, colors, and smells. Finally, **chlorine** or another chemical is added to the water to get rid of any harmful bacteria. Since the water is now clear and treated, it can now flow into a river or stream without harming the living things around it.

Read each question. Circle the letter of the best answer.

1. What would be the effect of dumping sewer water into rivers or the ocean?

   A We would run out of water.

   B Nothing bad would happen.

   C It would pollute the plants and animals near the water.

   D Bacteria would eat the sewage.

2. Why is wastewater processed?

   A to keep it smelly

   B to make it safe to return to nature

   C to add bacteria

   D to use excess chlorine that would be wasted

3. What is the purpose of the screen in the process?

   A to catch solid objects in the water

   B to keep out animals and plants

   C to let pollution out of the water

   D to put bacteria into the water

4. What is the effect of the bacteria in the tank?

   A They get the odors out of the water.

   B They get large solid objects out of the water.

   C They break down the solid materials into stinky gases.

   D They kill bacteria.

5. Why is the water shaken with air?

   A The filter needs air to work.

   B The chlorine needs air to work.

   C The sand needs air to work.

   D The bacteria need air to work.

6. What is the effect of chlorine?

   A It makes the water clear.

   B It makes the water smell.

   C It gets rid of solids in the water.

   D It gets rid of bacteria.

7. As a result of the filtering —

   A the water can hurt plants and animals

   B the water is free of most bacteria, colors, and smells

   C we can take showers all day

   D bacteria can eat the sewage

8. On a separate sheet of paper, describe why water is allowed to flow back into rivers after the treatment process.

Before you begin this lesson, take this quiz to show what you know about using context clues. Read this passage about a strange object. Then answer the questions.

A WHAT?

Marissa peered at the top of the old library building. A scary-looking creature made from stone leaned over the edge of the rooftop.

"What's that?" she asked Mrs. Stanley, pointing.

"A gargoyle," Mrs. Stanley said.

"A what?" Marissa asked, but Mrs. Stanley was busy gathering the students and bringing them into the library. Marissa walked up to the front desk.

"What's that spooky thing on the roof?" she asked the librarian. "It has large wings and its stare is so <u>intense</u> that it feels like its eyes could pierce me!"

"That's a gargoyle," the librarian said. "It's a type of statue. Many years ago, builders put them on roofs to scare away evil spirits and keep buildings safe. The one we have is called a <u>griffin</u>."

The librarian brought Marissa to the <u>reference</u> section and showed her how to find "gargoyle" in the encyclopedia. There were pictures of gargoyles from around the world. Marissa tried to look up "griffin," but she didn't know how to spell it. She went outside and looked up at the statue again. Its body looked like a lion, but it had the head and wings of an eagle. It looked like it was doing a good job of <u>safeguarding</u> the library.

Circle the letter of the best answer.

1. What clue words help to explain the gargoyle's <u>intense</u> stare?

   A that spooky thing

   B It has large wings

   C its eyes could pierce me

   D It's a type of statue

2. If the gargoyle is <u>safeguarding</u> the library, what is it doing?

   A laughing at people as they walk by

   B watching customers enter the library

   C protecting the building

   D predicting the weather

3. A <u>griffin</u> is probably a type of —

   A eagle

   B monster

   C lion

   D encyclopedia

4. The <u>reference</u> section of the library would NOT contain —

   A biographies

   B dictionaries

   C encyclopedias

   D mysteries

You can find the meaning of an unfamiliar word by **using context clues. Context clues** are words or phrases that help you understand a new word.

To use context clues,

- Read the sentence or paragraph with the unfamiliar word.
- Look for surrounding words or phrases that tell you about the new word.
- Replace the unfamiliar word with a familiar word or phrase to see if it makes sense.

Here's How

Read these sentences. What context clues might tell you what *snapper* means?

Some people enjoy seafood with their sushi, such as tuna, <u>snapper</u>, yellowtail, or shrimp. Sometimes the seafood is cooked, and sometimes it is raw. The Japanese prefer to eat their seafood raw instead of cooked.

Think About It

1. *I see the unfamiliar word* <u>snapper</u>. *I also see the clue words* such as.

2. *Tuna is a familiar word that comes after* <u>such as</u>. *Tuna is an example of a type of seafood.*

3. *The unfamiliar word* <u>snapper</u> *also comes after* such as. *Therefore, snapper must be a type of seafood.*

Try This Strategy

Scan and Skim

When you **scan and skim,** you quickly look over a passage to see what it is about.

- Ask yourself, "What is the passage about?"
- Look at the title and any pictures to find out.
- Skim the passage quickly for important details.

Read the article. Use the Reading Guide for tips. The tips will help you scan and skim and use context clues as you read.

Reading Guide

Scan the article. Notice the title of the article.

Skim the text for any underlined words. Look for signal words and phrases like or, such as, *and in other words.*

Use the clue words to determine the meaning of new words as you read.

SUSHI

One kind of Japanese <u>cuisine</u> called sushi is a popular food that many people enjoy. Sushi is mostly made of sticky white rice mixed with vinegar. The rice may be rolled together with fish or vegetables. Then it is wrapped in salty, dried seaweed and cut into round slices. It is pretty to look at and pleasant to taste or, in other words, <u>savory</u>.

Some people enjoy seafood with their sushi, such as tuna, snapper, yellowtail, or shrimp. Sometimes the seafood is cooked, and sometimes it is raw. The Japanese <u>prefer</u> to eat their seafood raw instead of cooked. They believe cooking the seafood destroys the <u>subtle</u>, or hidden, flavors. No matter what, the seafood is always served very fresh. Sushi sometimes has vegetables too, such as <u>asparagus</u>, cucumbers, and carrots. The vegetables are sliced into long, thin strips so that they are easy to eat.

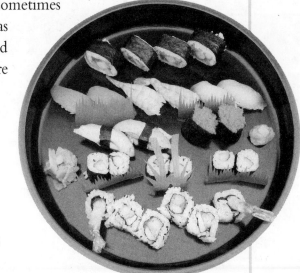

People like to dip their sushi in soy sauce. Then, they eat it with their fingers or with chopsticks. Any way you have it, it's delicious.

Now use what you learned to use context clues.

Answer the questions on the next page.

Practice using context clues in the article you just read.

EXAMPLE	Reread the sentence in which the word is found.
What are <u>asparagus</u>?	It starts with, "Sushi sometimes has vegetables too."
A seafood B seaweed C vegetables D sushi	**Notice words in the sentence that might help explain the unfamiliar word.** I see the clue words such as. **Use any clue words to understand the meaning of the unfamiliar word.** <u>Asparagus</u> is an example of a vegetable.

Now read each question. Circle the letter of the best answer.

1. In paragraph 2, what word gives a clue to the meaning of <u>subtle</u>?

   A fresh

   B raw

   C hidden

   D cooked

2. In this passage, the word <u>prefer</u> means —

   A to choose

   B to decline

   C to refuse

   D to dislike

3. In the first sentence, what do you think the word <u>cuisine</u> means?

   A sushi

   B popular

   C people

   D food

4. In the first paragraph, the clue words <u>pleasant to taste</u> refer to the word —

   A subtle

   B savory

   C delicate

   D traditional

NEWS FLASH!

SKATEBOARDER JUMPS OVER GREAT WALL OF CHINA

Way jumped the Great Wall of China five times.

BEIJING, CHINA—Thousands gathered in China to watch Danny Way skateboard over the Great Wall of China. He crossed the 61-foot distance by sliding down a long ramp at almost 50 miles an hour. He made it to the other side on his first try, though he <u>botched</u> the landing by falling on the ramp. Way made four more jumps over the wall, landing correctly each time.

Other people have tried to jump the Great Wall, but Way is the most successful so far. In 2002, a man died while trying to jump his bicycle over the wall. Way is no stranger to taking risks, however. In 1997, he became the first person to drop out of a helicopter and on top of a skateboard ramp. He created a new skateboarding phrase in the process: the Bomb Drop.

Way has been skateboarding since he was six years old. He holds the world record for the longest skateboarding jump at 79 feet. The **daring** skateboarder also set the world height record for a jump at 23 1/2 feet.

Write About It

Read this sentence from the article: "He made it to the other side on his first try, though he <u>botched</u> the landing by falling on the ramp." What does <u>botched</u> mean? Use the graphic organizer below to help you find the meaning.

Word		Clues		Meaning
botched	→		→	

Review

As you read, look for **context clues** to find the meanings of unfamiliar words. If you find an unfamiliar word, look for the words around it in the sentence or in the paragraph to help you understand its meaning.

Review the steps you can use to find context clues.

- Read the sentence or paragraph that has the unfamiliar word.
- Look for clue words that describe or explain the meaning of the word.
- Replace the unfamiliar word with a word you know. Does the sentence make sense?

Practice 1

Read the following passage. Use context clues to find the meaning of <u>meticulous</u>. Look for an explanation of the word or a comparison that can help you define it. Replace it with a word you know, and see if the sentence makes sense.

Reggie spent Saturday morning cleaning his room. It had been a while since he had cleaned, and he wanted his room to be spotless. He made his bed and picked up his laundry from the floor. Then he straightened his desk. He arranged all his papers neatly into folders and put his books back in his bookcase. He perfectly tucked his chair under his desk. Finally, Reggie dusted and vacuumed to give his room a clean, fresh feeling. Reggie is definitely <u>meticulous</u> when it comes to keeping his room neat!

Read through the paragraph again to find clue words that can help you define the word <u>meticulous</u>.

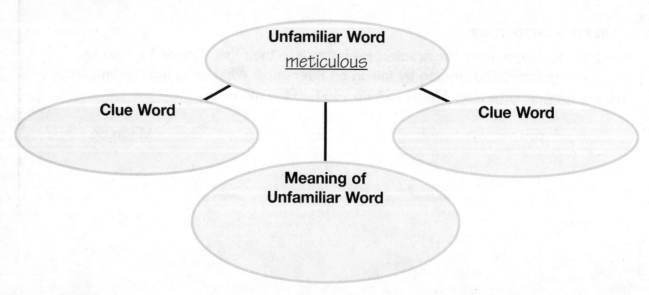

Unfamiliar Word
meticulous

Clue Word

Clue Word

Meaning of Unfamiliar Word

Practice 2

Read the passage. Use clue words to figure out the meaning of the words in italics.

People who are left-handed often feel <u>isolated</u>, or separated, from the rest of the world. They have to make many <u>adjustments</u> in everyday life just to operate successfully.

For example, lefties have to plan where to sit for family dinner <u>functions</u>. Otherwise, they might bump elbows with a righty. Lefties also have to use special scissors when cutting paper. When left-handed people write, they drag their hand across the fresh ink on the paper, smudging their words. Pencil works best for them. On a computer mouse, the <u>dominant</u> button, the one used the most, is on the left side. When lefties use the mouse with their left hand, they clumsily have to use their ring finger instead of their pointer finger.

Is it right for life to be so hard for lefties?

Use this graphic organizer to find the meanings of the underlined words.

Unfamiliar Word	Clue Words	Meaning
1.		
2.		
3.		
4.		

Practice 3

Read the passage. Then use context clues to answer the questions. Make a graphic organizer on a separate sheet of paper to organize your thoughts.

> Grandpa didn't like the trumpet. After Eric's school concert, he shrugged his shoulders, with his eyebrows <u>furrowed</u> and his lips <u>pursed</u>. "Too loud," he said. "Come play my violin. It has a beautiful sound."
>
> Eric rolled his eyes. After hesitating, he finally agreed. "Okay, I'll come play your violin."
>
> Grandpa had brought his violin with him all the way from Poland when he moved to America. Every weekend, he took it out and gently wiped it down with oil until it shined.
>
> That Sunday, Eric went over to Grandpa's tiny apartment. Grandpa <u>cautiously</u> carried the violin into the living room and set it on the coffee table. Its dark wooden body shone. Grandpa handed Eric the bow.
>
> "Go ahead," Grandpa encouraged. Eric scraped one of the strings with the bow, and the instrument **shrieked.** Grandpa came around behind him, took Eric's hands, and showed him how to move the bow smoothly over the strings. A deep, <u>resonant</u> sound came out of the violin.
>
> "Go on," said Grandpa. Eric moved the bow over the other strings, finding familiar notes but hearing them in unfamiliar ways. As the instrument sang, Grandpa gave a pleased nod.

1. If Grandpa's eyebrows are <u>furrowed</u> and his lips are <u>pursed</u>, how might he be feeling?

_____

_____

2. Grandpa carries the violin <u>cautiously</u>. Use what you know about how Grandpa treats the violin to tell what <u>cautiously</u> means.

_____

_____

3. Use clues from the passage and what you know about violins to define the word <u>resonant</u>.

_____

_____

Introduction

When you come upon an unfamiliar word, look for **context clues** to find the meaning.

As you saw on pages 55–57, graphic organizers can help you use context clues.

- In the first box, write the unfamiliar word.
- In the second box, write any clue words that help describe the unfamiliar word. These might be definitions, examples, or phrases that explain the difficult word.
- In the third box, write your own definition of the unfamiliar word.

Here's How

Read these sentences. Use the familiar words and sentences to understand the meaning of <u>impaired</u>.

Luckily, his **physical** health wasn't <u>impaired</u>. However, his mental health was affected, and Gage's personality changed. Before the accident, he was hardworking and amicable. After the accident, he was no longer the friendly person that people once knew.

Think About It

Word	Context Clues	Meaning
<u>impaired</u>	The word *wasn't* comes before the word <u>impaired</u>. His mental health *was* affected. The word *affected* means changed.	damaged or changed

Try This Strategy

Visualize

When you **visualize,** you picture what is going on.

- As you read, make a picture in your mind of the people, setting, and action.
- Create the scene in your mind with as much detail as possible.
- Imagine watching the story take place.

Read the article. Use the Reading Guide for tips that can help you visualize and use context clues as you read.

 Reading Guide

Visualize the description of the accident. How can a mental image help you understand the meaning of <u>penetrated</u>?

What words describe Gage's personality before the accident?

What words describe Gage's personality after the accident?

Why would doctors be fascinated by Gage's story? How does this help you understand what <u>peculiar</u> means?

THE BRAIN OF PHINEAS GAGE

On September 13, 1848, there was an explosion on a railroad construction site in Vermont. No one was killed, but one person was injured: a worker named Phineas Gage. He was struck in the head with a long metal tool. Incredibly, he awoke only moments after the accident occurred, appearing to be in better <u>condition</u> than expected. A doctor examined him, and Phineas soon returned to work.

Phineas Gage had not simply been hit in the head. The nearly four-foot-long tool had actually <u>penetrated</u> his skull. It entered at his cheekbone, passed straight through his head, and exited above his eye. The frontal lobe of Gage's brain was nearly destroyed.

Luckily, his physical health wasn't <u>impaired</u>. However, his mental health was affected, and Gage's personality changed. Before the accident, he was hardworking and <u>amicable</u>. After the accident, he was no longer the friendly person that people once knew. His moods were <u>erratic</u>, changing from happy to angry in a moment. His new <u>impulsive</u> behavior caused him to make sudden and careless decisions. He would do or say whatever he wanted, regardless of what other people thought.

Doctors became fascinated by Gage's <u>peculiar</u> case. At the time, people knew little about how the brain worked. Gage's injury, however, proved that the frontal lobe controlled emotion and decision-making. Gage's skull is preserved in a museum, and scientists continue to study it.

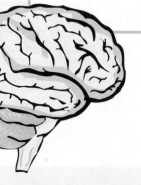

Answer the questions on the next page.

Practice using context clues by answering questions about the article you just read. Read each question. Circle the letter of the best answer.

1. In this passage, what does <u>peculiar</u> mean?

   A ordinary

   B unusual

   C typical

   D common

2. The context clues *passed straight through his head* tells you that <u>penetrated</u> means —

   A went through

   B hit

   C bounced

   D scratched up

3. What words from the text help to define the word <u>amicable</u>?

   A sudden and careless decisions

   B he was hardworking

   C He would do or say whatever he wanted

   D the friendly person that people once knew

4. What is an example of an <u>impulsive</u> person?

   A someone who is responsible and in control

   B someone who makes sudden and careless decisions

   C someone who is cautious and careful

   D someone who is alert and guarded

5. To be <u>erratic</u> is to —

   A change without warning

   B work hard

   C be kind

   D be healthy

6. Use context clues to find the meaning of the word <u>condition</u>. Write it on a separate sheet of paper.

ORANGUTAN TWINS BORN

The twins' full names are Pumpkin Pie and Peanut Butter.

MIAMI, FL—Parrot Jungle Island is seeing double. The park is now home to twin baby orangutans. They are the first set of orangutan twins born in captivity in the last 20 years.

The twin girls, Pumpkin and Peanut, were given their names in a "Name the Babies" contest at Parrot Jungle Island. The public first viewed the twins six months after they were born, as part of a "Twins Celebration" weekend. As part of the event, Parrot Jungle Island admitted twins, triplets, and quadruplets into the park for free.

Though Pumpkin and Peanut look almost identical, they are actually fraternal twins. In addition to one being bigger than the other, the two sisters also have different personalities. Pumpkin tends to be more adventurous, while Peanut is more cautious. They even have different tastes in food. One likes apples and pears while the other likes bananas.

Orangutans normally live in tropical rain forests. Because they are <u>endangered</u>, orangutans like Pumpkin and Peanut often live protected in parks and zoos.

Pumpkin and Peanut can continue to be seen living happily on Parrot Jungle Island, though they won't be babies much longer.

Write About It

In the fourth paragraph, the author says that orangutans are <u>endangered</u>. What does the term <u>endangered</u> mean in this sentence? Write a paragraph of your own using the word <u>endangered</u>.

Show What You Learned

Read this article about sleepwalking. Then answer the questions on the next page.

Sleepwalking

A teenage boy wakes up in the shower with his hand full of shampoo. A woman wakes up outside her house with her keys in her hand. She is wearing her nightgown, and it's four o'clock in the morning. At a sleepover, a girl sits up with her eyes open and asks where her dog went. Her friends look at her strangely. The girl has been asleep for more than an hour.

These people are all suffering from **somnambulism,** or sleepwalking. Sleepwalking happens to children more often than to adults, and to males more than to females. Most children outgrow sleepwalking when they grow up. However, it can also happen to adults who experience an <u>overabundance</u> of stress and anxiety. Therefore, when a person is relaxed, sleepwalking does not usually occur.

In cartoons, sleepwalkers are usually seen walking around with their eyes closed and their arms out in front of them. In reality, most sleepwalkers keep their eyes open, though they may look dazed. They may even talk, or <u>interact</u>, with people. Some sleepwalkers can appear so alert that it can be difficult for others to know that they are, in fact, asleep!

Many people believe that it is dangerous to wake sleepwalkers, but that is a <u>myth</u>. Sleepwalkers have been known to injure themselves by falling down stairs, tripping on furniture in the house, or even getting in car accidents! People should gently guide sleepwalkers back to bed or wake them <u>gingerly</u>. Waking them quickly is too startling and can cause them to become frightened. When sleepwalkers do wake up, they are usually confused, or <u>disoriented</u>.

Lately, sleepwalking has been in the news. A few people have been <u>acquitted</u> of crimes because they claimed that they were asleep when they committed them. One man even claimed that he was not guilty of murder, because he was asleep while he did the killing!

Read each question. Circle the letter of the best answer.

1. In paragraph 2, another way to say
   <u>overabundance</u> is —

   A some

   B small amount

   C huge amount

   D not any

2. What context clue helps you to
   understand the meaning of <u>gingerly</u>?

   A They are usually confused.

   B It is dangerous to wake sleepwalkers.

   C Most sleepwalkers keep their eyes
   open.

   D Waking them quickly is too startling.

3. In paragraph 4, the word <u>gingerly</u>
   means —

   A carefully

   B aggressively

   C usually

   D forcefully

4. What does <u>disoriented</u> mean?

   A fatigued

   B confused

   C injured

   D experienced

5. In paragraph 3, what context clue gives
   you the meaning of <u>interact</u>?

   A Sleepwalkers keep their eyes open.

   B They may even talk.

   C Sleepwalkers can appear so alert.

   D They may look dazed.

6. From reading the context clues, it is
   clear that, in this passage, the word
   <u>myth</u> means —

   A false

   B dangerous

   C true

   D safe

7. What clue words help you understand
   the meaning of <u>acquitted</u>?

   A confused

   B not guilty

   C asleep

   D committed

8. On a separate sheet of paper, write a
   definition for the word <u>interact</u>. Use
   context clues from the passage.

Show What You Know

Before you begin this lesson, take this quiz to show what you know about identifying main ideas and details. Read the passage, then answer the questions.

Mysteries of the Sun

It gives us the energy we use to eat, drive our cars, and make electricity. It is responsible for all life on Earth. It's the brightest thing in the sky. The Sun, however, still holds many mysteries.

As it burns, the Sun pours out **radiation,** such as light and heat. It also pours out trillions of tiny **particles** called neutrinos. These particles are very small. They're so tiny that they can pass through anything, day and night. Millions of them are pouring through your body right now. Neutrinos pass right through Earth and out the other side. Scientists still aren't sure what they are.

Here's another strange fact about the Sun. The air around it is hotter than its surface! The surface of the Sun is about 11,000 degrees Fahrenheit but the atmosphere is a scorching *3,000,000* degrees Fahrenheit! That's like the air above your stove being hotter than the burner! Again, scientists are not sure why this might be.

Circle the letter of the best answer.

1. Which sentence best states the main idea of the passage?

   A The Sun pours out many tiny particles.

   B The Sun has many mysteries.

   C The Sun's atmosphere is hotter than its surface.

   D The Sun is the brightest thing in the sky.

2. The main idea of the last paragraph is best stated by the —

   A first sentence

   B second sentence

   C fourth sentence

   D last sentence

3. The sentence *These particles are very small* supports the idea that —

   A the Sun is hot

   B the Sun gives us energy

   C the Sun's atmosphere is hotter than the surface

   D the Sun releases trillions of particles

4. Which detail supports the main idea of the last paragraph?

   A The Sun is mysterious.

   B The Sun's atmosphere is 3 million degrees.

   C The Sun is responsible for life on Earth.

   D Neutrinos can pass through anything.

Introduction

When you **identify main ideas and details**, you pick out important ideas or events in a passage and the smaller facts and details that support them.

To identify main ideas and details in a paragraph or a whole passage,

- Read the passage or paragraph. Think about what it is mostly about.
- Find the main idea or event. The main idea is often stated in the title, in the first sentence, or in the first or last paragraph.
- Look for details that answer *who, what, where, when,* and *why* about the main idea.

Here's How

Read this paragraph. What is the main idea?

Suddenly, the lights dimmed. They faded away until nothing but a dull brown light glowed from the lamps. Mandy heard her baby brother start to whimper.

Think About It

1. The paragraph tells about something happening to the lights.

2. The first sentence tells what happens. The lights turned dim. This is the main idea.

3. The other sentences tell how the lights dim and what happens as a result. These sentences provide details that tell about, or support, the main idea.

Try This Strategy

Predict

When you **predict,** you look for clues and make a guess about what you will read or what will happen next.

- Before you read the passage, read the title and look at the pictures. They will give you an idea of what the passage might be about.
- As you read, predict what might happen next.
- Check your predictions. Were they correct? Revise them as you continue to read.

Read the passage. Use the Reading Guide for tips. The tips will help you predict and identify main ideas and details as you read.

Reading Guide

The title and the picture of a light bulb are clues that this story will be about light or electricity.

Something strange is happening in the story. The clues to what is happening are details that support the main idea.

Predict the ending. Imagine what might be causing the lights to brighten and dim.

Think about what this story is about. The main idea tells what is causing the strange events in the story.

STRANGE POWER

It started with an odd hum. At first, Mandy could barely hear it over the freezing rain falling on the windows. But the hum got louder. As it did, the room seemed to brighten.

"Are you doing that?" her mom called from the kitchen. The lights in the house were getting brighter and brighter.

"No. What's happening?" Mandy shouted back. She jumped up and ran to the kitchen. Mom had the refrigerator door open. Light was pouring out as if the fridge were opening to another world. The motor buzzed and hummed like an engine.

Suddenly, the lights dimmed. They faded away until nothing but a dull brown light glowed from the lamps. Mandy heard her baby brother start to **whimper.**

She opened the front door and looked down the street. The lights began to brighten again. What she saw next amazed her. A tree had fallen against the power lines, and it was slowly bouncing. As the tree bounced downward, the lights grew dim. As the tree rose, the lights blazed bright again.

Now use what you learned to identify the main idea and details.

Answer the questions on the next page.

Practice identifying the main ideas and details of the passage you just read.

EXAMPLE

What is the main idea of the first paragraph?

A The room seemed to get brighter.

B It was raining outside.

C An odd hum came over the house.

D The hum grew louder.

Review the paragraph to find out what it is mostly about.

The paragraph tells about a humming sound and the room getting brighter.

Look for the most important event.

The most important event is that the house started humming.

Find details that tell about the main idea.

The room brightening and the hum growing louder tell about the odd hum. The main idea is that an odd hum came over the room.

Now read each question. Circle the letter of the best answer.

1. Which detail supports the idea that the lights are getting brighter?

    A The lamps gave off only a dull brown glow.

    B A tree had fallen on the power lines.

    C Light was pouring out of the refrigerator.

    D Mandy went into the kitchen.

2. Which sentence tells a detail that supports the main idea of the fourth paragraph?

    A Mandy was confused.

    B The bulbs only gave a brown glow.

    C Light poured from the fridge.

    D Mandy has a baby brother.

3. What is the main idea of the last paragraph?

    A Mandy was amazed by what she saw on the street.

    B The lights were brightening and growing dim again.

    C A tree had fallen across the power lines and was affecting the lights.

    D Mandy looked down the street.

4. What is the main idea or event of the passage?

    A Mandy's baby brother whimpers.

    B Mandy's mother opens the refrigerator.

    C Mandy is confused.

    D A tree falls on the power lines, causing the lights to change.

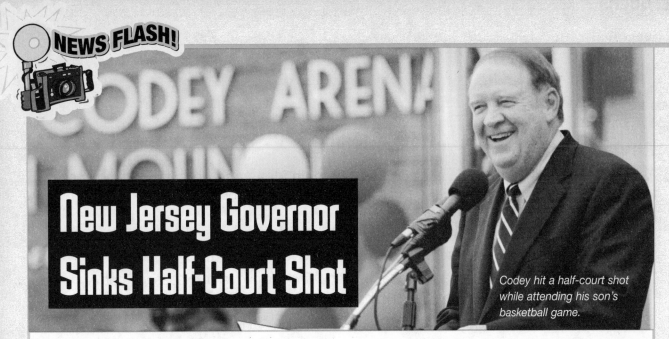

NEWS FLASH!

New Jersey Governor Sinks Half-Court Shot

Codey hit a half-court shot while attending his son's basketball game.

EAST RUTHERFORD, NJ—Now that's what they call a long shot! Richard J. Codey became the first active New Jersey governor to hit a half-court shot at a high school basketball game. Codey, now a state senator, won two tickets to a New Jersey Nets game for making the difficult shot.

Codey attended the game to watch his son play. He got a chance to take the shot at halftime, when the $1 raffle ticket he bought came up a winner.

When the basket went in, Codey acted like any athlete would. He dropped to one knee, pumped his fist, and even high-fived his wife. "I saw it [the shot] was right on," said Codey afterward. "Ninety-nine out of 100 people are short with the shot."

Codey is no stranger to basketball. He is a huge basketball fan and a youth basketball coach. He even sank another half-court shot at a basketball tournament four years earlier.

The governor, who already had season tickets to New Jersey Nets games, donated the tickets to someone who had never been to a professional basketball game.

Write About It

Now practice the skill using a real news story. Complete this graphic organizer. First, write the sentence that shows the main idea of this article. Then identify three details in the article that tell more about the main idea.

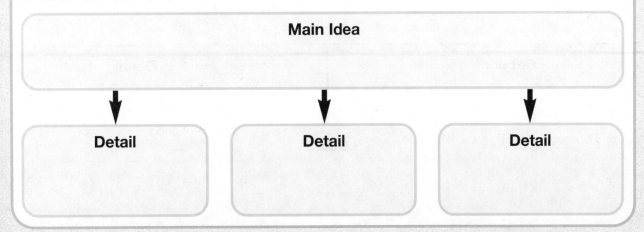

Main Idea

↓   ↓   ↓

Detail   **Detail**   **Detail**

LESSON

5

Identifying Main
Ideas and Details

Ladder to Success

Review

As you read, it is important to be able to **identify main ideas and details.** Once you have found a main idea, you can search for facts or events that support it.

Review the steps that help identify main ideas and details.

- Read the passage or paragraph, and think about what it is mostly about.
- Decide on the most important idea or event. The main idea of a passage can sometimes be found in the title, the beginning, or the ending.
- Ask *who, what, where, when,* and *why* about the main idea to find supporting details.

Practice 1

Read the following passage. After you read, look at the first and last sentences to find the main idea. Then ask questions about the main idea to find supporting details.

> Matt didn't think anyone would like the school play. All the actors seemed really nervous. Their costumes were just dress-up clothes that they had brought from home. The set had been built in a hurry, and he thought it looked sloppy. Plus, during their dress rehearsal, four students had messed up their lines. As Matt heard the audience taking their seats, he took a deep breath.

Using the chart below, write the main idea in the top oval. Write the supporting details in the ovals below it.

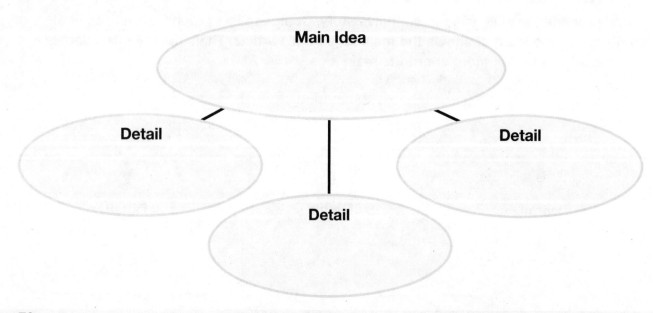

70

Practice 2

Read the passage. What are the main idea and details?

Sandra tried to concentrate, but the guitar was just too noisy. She was already letting Gretchen and her band use more than half the basement. With all the girls playing at once, the racket was too loud for her to focus on her painting. The only other place for her to go was the dusty garage.

First, Sandra swept piles of dust and trash into a bin. Next, she dragged all her stuff out of the basement. She picked up her paints and **easel** and carried them away from the pounding noise. Then she went back for her brushes, rags, and water. Here in the garage, it was cool and quiet. She could hear the traffic rumbling far away. She might learn to like it out here.

Use this graphic organizer to identify the main idea and details.

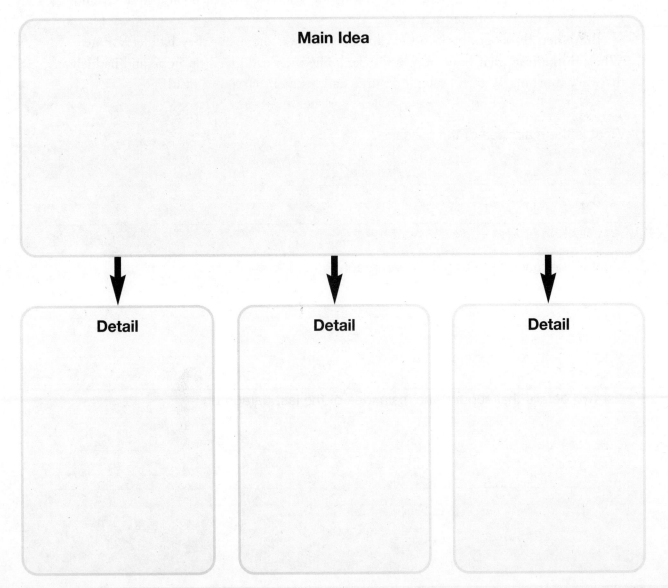

Main Idea

Detail

Detail

Detail

Practice 3

Read the passage. Then identify the main idea and details to answer the questions. Make a graphic organizer on a separate sheet of paper to organize your thoughts.

There are a million ways to die in the Australian Outback. The Outback is a scorching desert stretching across most of western Australia. Few roads or landmarks break up the landscape. Fresh water is **scarce,** and food is almost nonexistent.

Many of the first explorers of the Outback met with tragedy. In 1860, the Irish explorer Robert O'Hara Burke and his party of explorers were the first to cross the great southern continent of Australia. He prepared by packing thousands of pounds of supplies onto horses and camels.

The group quickly became exhausted. Burke decided that the entire party couldn't make it across the desert. He left most of his men and supplies at a camp near a creek. He and a few other men crossed the entire continent on their own. Their supplies began to **dwindle** rapidly as they made the return journey. They had to reach camp quickly and reunite with the rest of the party.

But when Burke got back to the camp, no one was there, but they had left a note. When Burke read their note, he was shocked. The men had given up hope and had left that very morning. With no supplies, Burke and his men starved to death.

1. What is the main idea of the passage?

   _____

   _____

2. What is the main idea of the last paragraph?

   _____

   _____

3. List two details that support the main idea of the last paragraph.

   _____

   _____

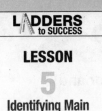
Guided Instruction 2

Introduction

The **main idea** of a passage is the most important idea or event. It is what the passage is mostly about. A paragraph can also have a main idea. Each main idea is supported by lesser facts or events called **details.**

As you saw on pages 69–71, graphic organizers help identify main idea and details.

- Review the passage or paragraph and decide what it is mostly about.
- Identify the main idea and write it in the first box. The main idea might be found in the title, the first sentence, the first paragraph, or the last paragraph.
- Look for facts and ideas that tell more about the main idea. Write these details in the other boxes.

Here's How

Read this paragraph. What are three details that support the main idea?

The simplest kind of advertising is called the "hard sell." This kind of advertising simply tells you that the product is a good product at a good price and that you should buy it. A hard sell for candy might tell you that it tastes great or comes in many flavors.

Think About It

Main idea	
The simplest advertising is the "hard sell."	**Detail:** Tells you the product is good
	Detail: Tells you the price is good
	Detail: Might tell you a candy tastes great

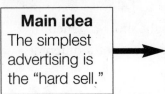

Monitor and Clarify

When you **monitor and clarify,** you make sure you understand what you read.

- Ask yourself whether you understand the ideas in each paragraph.
- Try restating the main ideas in your own words to make sure you understand them.
- Reread any section that you do not understand.

Read the article. Use the Reading Guide for tips. These tips can help you monitor and clarify and identify main ideas and details as you read.

 Reading Guide

State the main idea of the first paragraph in your own words.

Look for details. What facts tell more about "hard sell" advertising?

Did you understand how "bandwagon advertising" is different from the "hard sell"?

Think about what you have read. Restate the main idea of the whole passage in your own words.

Analyzing Advertising

You see and hear advertising almost every day—on TV, radio, in magazines, even on buses or on billboards. Advertising can be beautiful, interesting, or funny. But never forget that advertising is trying to get you to buy something.

The simplest kind of advertising is called the "hard sell." This kind of advertising simply tells you that the product is a good product at a good price and that you should buy it. A hard sell for candy might tell you that it tastes great or comes in many flavors.

Another kind of advertising is called "bandwagon advertising." This advertising tells you that lots of people are buying the product, so you should, too. A bandwagon ad for candy tells you that all your friends are buying this candy. If you want to be like them, you should buy it, too.

One of the sneakiest types of advertising is an anti-advertisement. These advertisements make fun of other ads, or they make fun of advertising itself. They seem to say, "We know that you're too smart to fall for advertising." An anti-advertisement for candy might show a bunch of foolish people seeing an advertisement for a different candy, then running out and buying it. Meanwhile, a smart person looks on, shaking her head and enjoying the candy that is actually being advertised.

Answer the questions on the next page.

Practice the Skill 2

Practice identifying main ideas and details by answering questions about the article you just read. Read each question. Circle the letter of the best answer.

1. Choose the main idea that is supported by this detail: *An anti-advertisement sometimes makes fun of advertising itself.*

   A One of the sneakiest types of advertisement is the anti-advertisement.

   B Anti-advertisements can make fun of other ads.

   C Advertising can be funny.

   D The simplest kind of advertisement is called the "hard sell."

2. Which detail supports the main idea that the bandwagon is a method of advertising?

   A Advertisers are trying to sell something.

   B This advertising says that if other people buy a candy bar, you should too.

   C This advertising tells you that a product is good.

   D A smart person looks on.

3. The main ideas in paragraphs 2, 3, and 4 are placed —

   A at the end of the passage

   B at the end of each paragraph

   C at the beginning of each paragraph

   D in the middle of each paragraph

4. What is the main idea of the whole article?

   A Advertising is trying to sell you something.

   B One type of advertising is the hard sell.

   C Bandwagon advertising tells you that other people are buying a product.

   D The sneakiest type of advertising is anti-advertising.

5. One clue to the main idea of the article is in —

   A the third paragraph

   B the title

   C the last sentence

   D the second paragraph

6. On a separate sheet of paper, create a chart showing the main idea of the passage and the main idea of each paragraph.

Thousands of cheering fans attended the robotics competition.

BRONX STUDENTS WIN ROBOT CONTESTS

NEW YORK, NY—A group of Bronx high school students are building robots and winning contests. Students from the Morris Campus Schools and the Bronx Aerospace Academy have achieved several victories in the FIRST Robotics Competition. FIRST stands for "For Inspiration and Recognition of Science Technology."

About 25,000 students on almost 1,000 teams compete in the robot-building event. The competition is more like a sporting event, and it features pep bands, cheerleaders, and flashing lights. Thousands of fans show up to cheer on the robots and their creators. The robots perform several tasks, including moving colored balls to score points and balancing seesawing platforms.

The Bronx students get some help designing and building their robots. Every year, engineers from Columbia University help the students shape the masses of wires and levers into working robots.

The winning team was crowned FIRST regional champions in 2003 and 2005. To recognize their success, the New York Yankees baseball team sponsored them. The Yankees honored them on the field at Yankee Stadium and offered free ball game tickets to the students.

Awards and baseball tickets are a nice bonus, but student Jairo Bastilla signed up because he liked the idea of building a robot. "It just sounded pretty cool to me," Bastilla said.

Write About It

Write a paragraph summarizing this article. Write the main idea in the first sentence. Then write three or four sentences stating details that support the main idea.

Read this article about powerful earthquakes. Then answer the questions on the next page.

An Earth-Shaking Event

California experiences earthquakes all the time. Alaska has been home to some of the most powerful earthquakes ever recorded. Volcanic Hawaii is full of earthquake rumblings. But some of the strongest earthquakes in United States history were nowhere near these places. They were centered in the town of New Madrid, Missouri. These earthquakes shook the country with amazing force, and it could happen again.

On December 18, 1811, the Midwest rocked with the force of an earthquake measuring 7.7 on the Richter scale. Over the next few months, three more giant quakes shook the area. Scientists think the final one may have registered over 9.0 on the Richter scale, making it much larger than the earthquake that destroyed San Francisco in 1906.

At the time, the Midwest was not heavily populated, so there were few **fatalities.** But that does not mean that the quakes were not noticed. The quakes destroyed buildings in St. Louis, and log cabins collapsed near Cincinnati, Ohio. The rumblings were felt as far away as New York City. Churches in Boston, Massachusetts, shook so hard that their bells rang.

Closer by, the quakes changed the course of the Mississippi River. The quake caused the river to flow backward, and when the flow returned to normal, the shape of the river had changed. Entire houses were swallowed by cracks in the earth.

Since the 1970s, scientists have been monitoring the area where the New Madrid earthquakes took place. They have recorded thousands of small earthquakes there. Most of the quakes are too small to be felt. But scientists say that there is a good chance that another major earthquake will shake the Midwest.

Unlike California, the Midwest is not prepared for the possibility of a large earthquake. The buildings there are not built to withstand shaking. Schools do not have earthquake drills. The emergency services, such as the fire department, have not trained for earthquake rescues. With the strong chance that another earthquake will strike the Midwest, citizens should begin to prepare.

Read each question. Circle the letter of the best answer.

1. The title suggests that the main idea of this passage might be —

   A California

   B earthquakes

   C scientists

   D the Midwest

2. What is the main idea of the last paragraph?

   A The Midwest is not prepared for large earthquakes.

   B Powerful earthquakes can occur in the Midwest.

   C Schools do not have earthquake drills.

   D California is prepared for earthquakes.

3. The main idea of the third paragraph is —

   A church bells rang in Boston

   B the Mississippi River flowed backward

   C the shaking was felt very far away

   D few people lived in the Midwest

4. Which detail supports the idea that the earthquake affected the Midwest in many ways?

   A Scientists have been monitoring the area.

   B There were few fatalities.

   C The Midwest is not prepared.

   D The Mississippi River was knocked off course.

5. The details in the second paragraph support the main idea that —

   A earthquakes happen all over the United States

   B more earthquakes may happen soon

   C the area is not prepared for quakes

   D the Midwest earthquakes were very powerful

6. A good way to restate the main idea of the entire article is —

   A the Midwest earthquakes had few fatalities

   B powerful earthquakes can happen in the Midwest

   C California has powerful earthquakes

   D thousands of small earthquakes have happened in the Midwest

7. Which detail answers a *where* question about the main idea of the article?

   A The quake measured over 9.0 on the Richter scale.

   B The earthquake shook the tiny town of New Madrid, Missouri.

   C California often experiences earthquakes.

   D Log cabins collapsed near Cincinnati, Ohio.

8. On a separate sheet of paper, restate the main idea of the article in your own words, and provide details to answer *who, what, where, when,* and *why.*

Before you begin this lesson, take this quiz to show what you know about drawing conclusions. Read this story about a strange new pet. Then answer the questions.

A Changeable Pet

Today, I brought home a new pet lizard. The sign in the shop window said the lizard could change color from green to yellow. I didn't believe it. When I got home, I put him in his **aquarium**. I added a dish of water and a special rock that stays warm all the time. Then I put some crickets into the aquarium. My sister asked what the crickets were for, but I didn't tell her. While she was **pestering** me, the lizard climbed onto the warm rock and turned bright yellow. Wow!

We wanted to see it turn green again. I took the lizard out of the aquarium and held him in my hands. Nothing happened. So, I let him loose on the cold kitchen floor. He turned green right away. Then I heard Mom coming down the hall. I scooped up the lizard and put him back in the aquarium.

My sister and I watched the lizard change color for a while longer. She still wanted to know why I put the crickets in there. After supper, we checked on my new pet. The crickets were gone. My sister gasped. She finally figured out what they were for!

Circle the letter of the best answer.

1. When the lizard gets warm, it —

   A turns yellow

   B turns green

   C eats a cricket

   D jumps onto the floor

2. In the second paragraph, when the writer says, "Nothing happened," he means the lizard did not —

   A change color

   B eat

   C move

   D jump onto the floor

3. Why did the writer scoop up the lizard?

   A He thought the lizard was cold and wanted to warm it up.

   B He didn't think his mother would want it on the kitchen floor.

   C He thought the lizard was hungry.

   D He was bored watching the lizard.

4. What are the crickets for?

   A They keep the lizard company.

   B They keep the aquarium clean.

   C They are the writer's other pets.

   D They are food for the lizard.

A **conclusion** is a reasonable judgment you form based on details you read.

To draw a conclusion,

- First think about what you already know about a subject.
- Then think about what you learn by reading.
- Put them together to make a reasonable judgment.

Here's How

Read these paragraphs. Draw a conclusion about what the speaker's job is.

> I stopped my patrol car when the call came in. It was 5:30 pm, just after sunset. Bright lights were coming on everywhere. The city looked busy.
>
> The radio crackled. I heard my **dispatcher's** voice. "Head over to the west side," Al said. "125th Street. A woman just called. She says a **cougar** jumped into her basement."

Think About It

1. I know that police officers have equipment like patrol cars and radios. I also know that police officers protect people.

2. I can tell by reading that the speaker has a patrol car and a radio. I also read that the speaker has to look for a cougar.

3. I can conclude that the speaker is a police officer.

Try This Strategy

Visualize

When you **visualize,** you picture in your mind what you are reading.

- Carefully read how the writer describes a person, place, thing, or event.
- Think about the details and specific words the writer uses. Use those details to form a mental image.
- Imagine a story taking place as if it were a movie in your mind.

Read the story. Use the Reading Guide for tips that can help you visualize and draw conclusions as you read.

Reading Guide

Picture the setting that is described. Then picture where a cougar might live. This is not a place where someone would expect to find a cougar.

Form a mental image of Bob talking to Al. Imagine what Bob looks like as Al answers.

Think about the details. Picture what Bob sees.

Notice the clues: the animal growls, the hair on Bob's neck stands up, and the animal is not a dog.

Basement Beastie

I stopped my patrol car when the call came in. It was 5:30 pm, just after sunset. Bright lights were coming on everywhere. The city looked busy.

The radio crackled. I heard my dispatcher's voice. "Head over to the west side," Al said. "125th Street. A woman just called. She says a cougar jumped into her basement."

"I'm sure it's just a dog," I said, shaking my head.

"You can tell her that when you get there, Bob," he said. "She swears it's a cougar."

I found the address and parked my car. A woman was on the stoop, holding a broom. She pointed at a broken window on the side of the building. "It went in there!" she shouted. I chuckled. If it had really been a cougar, that broom sure wasn't going to keep her safe.

I grabbed my flashlight and knelt next to the window. "Here?" I asked. She nodded. As I peered in, I heard a low growl. The hair on my neck stood up. This was no dog.

Now use what you already know and what you learned to draw conclusions.

Answer the questions on the next page.

Practice the Skill 1

Practice drawing conclusions about the story you just read.

EXAMPLE

What conclusion can you draw about how Bob feels when he says, "I'm sure it's just a dog"?

A Bob thinks dogs are funny.

B Bob wants Al to be his friend.

C Bob doesn't believe she saw a cougar.

D Bob wants to cover up the fact that he's scared.

Think about things you already know as you read.

I know that people shake their heads when they think something is wrong.

Review the passage to find details.

When I reread this part of the passage, I can form a mental image of Bob shaking his head when he answers Al.

Combine the details in the passage with what you already know.

I think Bob believes the woman is wrong.

Now read each question. Circle the letter of the best answer.

1. The woman is holding the broom —

   A to protect herself from the cougar

   B to clean up the front stoop

   C to show it to Bob

   D to lean on like a crutch

2. When does Bob change his opinion about what the woman probably saw?

   A when he gets the call from Al

   B when he sees the broom the woman is holding

   C when he arrives in the neighborhood

   D when he hears the animal growl

3. Which sentence supports the conclusion that Bob became scared when he looked in the window?

   A "It went in there!" she shouted.

   B The hair on my neck stood up.

   C I stopped my patrol car when the call came in.

   D As I peered in, I heard a low growl.

4. If the story continues, what is most likely to happen next?

   A Bob sees a dog.

   B Bob sees a cougar.

   C Bob jumps into the basement.

   D Bob leaves without helping.

Python Bursts After Swallowing Alligator

The Burmese python with a dead alligator sticking out of its stomach.

MIAMI, FL—Talk about an upset stomach! A 13-foot Burmese python split in two when it tried to swallow a 6-foot alligator. The dead bodies of both animals were found in Everglades National Park by a helicopter pilot and wildlife researcher.

The snake was found with half the gator sticking out of its stomach. Scientists say the alligator may have clawed at the python's stomach as the snake tried to swallow it.

This is the fourth known deadly gator-python meeting in the past three years. In other cases, the alligator won, or the battle killed both animals. Pythons were introduced to the Everglades when people began dumping their pet snakes in the swamps. Scientists had hoped that the exotic pets would be no match for the alligators that lived in the swamps. But this recent discovery proves that pythons are a growing problem.

Write About It

Now you will practice the skill using a real news story. Complete this graphic organizer by filling in the first two boxes that lead to this conclusion.

What I Already Know	What I Learned	Conclusion
		Pythons are a growing problem in the Everglades.

Review

As you read, you can **draw a conclusion**. Use things you already know and clues and details the writer provides. Combine these together to make a decision or form an idea about characters, events, and situations.

Review the steps you can use to draw a conclusion.

- Think about things you already know about a topic.
- Note the details and clues as you read.
- Combine details from the text with things you know.

Practice 1

Read the following story. As you read, think about what you already know about owning a pet. Think about how a dog would greet you when you come home from school. Then look for clues in the story that help you draw a conclusion about what happened to Peanut.

> When Dina came home from school, the gate to the yard was open. Dina called Peanut, her dog, to go for their daily walk around the block. Peanut did not come. Dina did not see Peanut anywhere in the yard. She went into the house and called Peanut's name. She did not hear the usual barking. Dina saw Peanut's leash hanging on the back of the kitchen door. Dina heard the TV on upstairs. She ran upstairs to find her mother.

Using the chart below, combine what you already know with clues from the story to draw a conclusion about what happened to Peanut.

What I Know	
Story Clues	
Conclusion	

Practice 2

Read the passage. What conclusion can you draw about what the children saw?

It was a beautiful spring day after a long winter. The buds were just beginning to open on the trees that ringed the schoolyard. Birds chirped in the trees and flew overhead as they built their nests.

Cora and Erica were playing ball in the schoolyard when they heard a big "thump!" Something had hit the building and fluttered to the ground. The girls stopped their game and went to see what made the noise. "It must have hit the window," said Cora.

"We should take it to Mr. Santos. He'll know how to fix a broken wing," said Erica.

Use this graphic organizer to draw a conclusion about what the children were looking at.

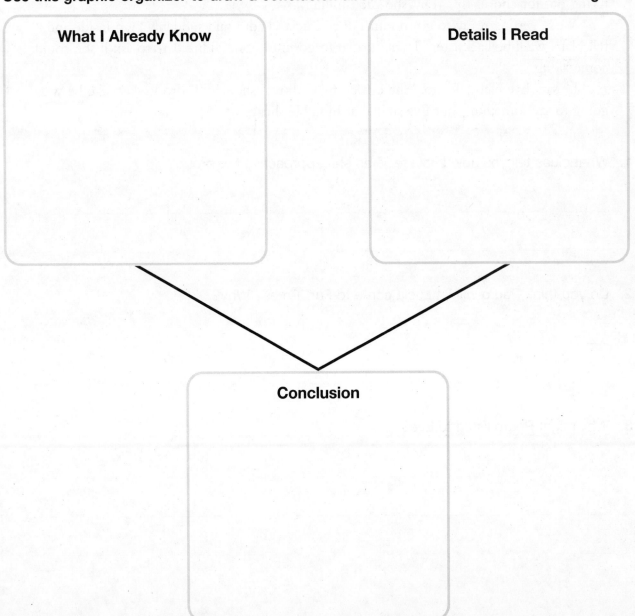

What I Already Know

Details I Read

Conclusion

Practice 3

Read the passage. Then draw conclusions to answer the questions. Make a graphic organizer on a separate sheet of paper to organize your thoughts.

Pedro and his friends sat on the stoop playing music. Lucia, Pedro's younger sister, paused behind the front door. She wanted to make it seem like she was just on her way out. But she really wanted to join Pedro's group. Pedro was always telling her to find her own friends.

"Hey, Pedro," she said, coming outside and standing on the top step. Pedro nodded silently without looking up. A couple of the other kids nodded at her, but no one moved to give her a place to sit down.

Eve, the girl that Pedro liked, was always nice to Lucia. "Hi, Lucia. I heard you were trying out for chorus this year," she said, smiling.

"We're getting ready to go to Fun Times, Lucia," Pedro said suddenly. "Go inside and tell Nana we'll be back later." Lucia turned to go inside. She didn't dare to ask if she could come along.

She saw Eve elbow Pedro. "She can come with us!" she said. Pedro looked like he was going to say something, but Eve smiled at him. He shrugged.

1. What clues tell you how Lucia feels as she approaches the group?

   _____

   _____

2. Do you think Pedro will let Lucia come to Fun Times? Why?

   _____

   _____

3. Why might Pedro listen to Eve?

   _____

   _____

   _____

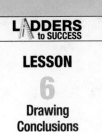
Introduction

Sometimes a writer does not state things directly about characters, events, and situations. Instead a writer gives clues and details. To **draw a conclusion,** you can combine these clues and hints with what you already know. The idea you form is a **conclusion.**

As seen on pages 83–85, graphic organizers help you draw conclusions.

- In the first box, write things you already know about the subject.
- In the second box, write details you learned by reading.
- Write your conclusion in the last box.

Here's How

Read these two sentences. What is one conclusion you can draw about the danger of giant African land snails?

> Giant African land snails multiply quickly if they get out into the wild. Their **extraordinary** appetites make them a threat to farm crops.

Think About It

What I Already Know		What I Learned		Conclusion
An animal's appetite means "how much it can eat."	→	Snails' appetites make them a threat to crops.	→	Giant African land snails could threaten the food supply.

Try This Strategy

Predict

Here's another strategy you can use to help draw conclusions. When you **predict,** you use what you have read and imagine what will happen next.

- When you begin, read the title and look at any pictures. Form an idea of what the passage will be about.
- Note the details the writer uses to describe people, places, and events. Ask yourself how these details give you clues about what will happen.
- Think about whether your predictions were correct. Make new predictions as you find out more.

Read the article. Use the Reading Guide for tips that can help you predict and draw conclusions as you read.

Reading Guide

Read the title and look at the picture. What do you think the article is about?

What might make a snail's appetite "extraordinary"? Have you ever seen something extraordinary?

What details in the article can you put together to predict what might happen if a giant land snail escaped?

Slime City

How big are giant African land snails? Their shells can grow up to ten inches long, and their bodies can stretch to fifteen long, slimy inches.

These creatures are becoming popular as pets in some parts of the world. But don't jump at the idea of owning one. These snails are illegal in the United States.

Sometimes called GALS, these **enormous** shell-dwellers are dangerous. Many of them are infected with a disease. It's called "rat lungworm," and it can make humans very sick.

Giant African land snails multiply quickly if they get out into the wild. Their extraordinary appetites make them a threat to farm crops. In the 1960s, Florida had to spend one million dollars to solve a GALS problem. To avoid a similar disaster, many states issued alerts in 2004. They warned people to be on the lookout for a snail **invasion.** Wisconsin issued so many alerts that the first half of the year was dubbed "The Great Snail Hunt of 2004." But it's not just Florida and Wisconsin that are on the alert. States from Maryland to Michigan worry about the snails.

If you know of a giant African land snail, report it to the proper authorities. Whatever you do, don't let it escape!

Answer the questions on the next page.

Practice drawing conclusions by answering questions about the story you just read. Read each question. Circle the letter of the best answer.

1. What conclusion can you draw from the information in the first paragraph?

   A The snails are extremely large.

   B The snails make good pets.

   C The snails are illegal.

   D The snails carry disease.

2. Which is a likely reason why it is illegal in the United States to own giant African land snails?

   A Their shells can grow up to 10 feet long.

   B They carry a disease that can make humans very sick.

   C Their bodies are slimy and can be stretched fifteen inches long.

   D Pets are hard to take care of.

3. Which best describes the conclusion the author wants readers to draw?

   A GALS make great pets but are difficult to take care of.

   B The government should change its laws about GALS.

   C People who are in contact with GALS should get rid of them immediately.

   D GALS are disgusting and owning them as pets is a bad idea.

4. According to the article, why would you not want a GALS as a pet?

   A They are ugly.

   B They carry disease.

   C They grow up to 15 inches long.

   D They move very slowly.

5. Based on the article, what is a reasonable conclusion you can draw about giant African land snails?

   A They won't eat the kinds of crops grown in Maryland or Michigan.

   B They eat a lot.

   C They are inexpensive to buy.

   D They only live in warm, rainy places.

6. On a separate sheet of paper, write a conclusion about what might happen if GALS escaped into the wild.

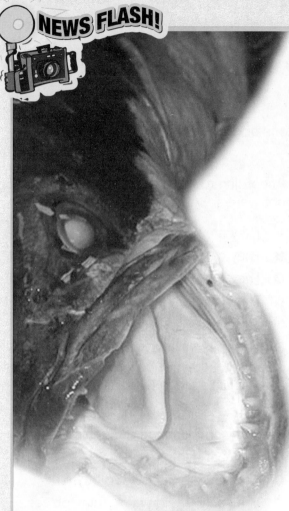

It's easy to see why some people have nicknamed these fish "Frankenfish."

Philly Fears Snakehead Invasion

PHILADELPHIA, PA—Strange fish caught in the Delaware River have people in Philadelphia scared. The fish, called snakehead fish, are unlike anything Philadelphians have ever seen before. The fish have razor-sharp teeth, have big appetites, and will try to eat just about anything. According to Gale Norton, Secretary of the U.S. Department of the Interior, snakeheads "are like something from a bad horror movie. They can eat **virtually** any small animal in their path."

Scientists say the fish will eat most of the animals they meet. Unlike other fish, snakeheads are able to crawl over land and live out of water for days. This lets them move from one body of water to another. They also have babies rapidly. Even a few snakeheads in a river or stream can quickly multiply. With nothing to stop them, snakeheads are a danger to many animals.

Snakeheads are new to the United States. Scientists think that people released them into ponds or rivers after they grew tired of keeping them as pets.

In China, this fish is common. There, snakeheads are said to have killed dogs and even people when their nests were threatened.

It seems people enjoy seeing movies about what frightens them. Several snakehead horror films have already been made. But many scientists say that the threat posed by snakeheads is not so bad. Some people think that nicknames like "Frankenfish" are unfair. Snakeheads may just be innocent creatures looking for a nice place to live.

Write About It

After reading this article, you might conclude that the snakehead fish can breathe air when it is out of water. How can you draw this conclusion? Write your answer on a separate sheet of paper. Include ideas you read in the article as well as what you already know.

Read this passage about cockroaches. Then answer the questions on the next page.

ROACHES ARE FOREVER

The cockroach is one of the hardiest animals on Earth. These insects live everywhere humans live. In fact, they need the same things we need: moisture, food, and warmth. They'll eat almost anything you and I eat, and they live in our snug, warm buildings year-round. You might find them creepy and disgusting, but cockroaches are masters of survival. Let's look at them more closely.

A cockroach can survive the radiation given off by a nuclear bomb and live for a week without its head. It will die only when it finally starves to death because it cannot eat without its mouth. A cockroach that is both blind and deaf can still find its way around by using its antennas. Those scary-looking hairs on a roach's legs and body can sense even the slightest movement of air, such as your foot coming down to step on it. When the roach senses danger, it can squeeze into a hiding space as thin as a dime. Don't bother trying to drown a cockroach—it can hold its breath underwater for over 40 minutes!

Cockroaches come out mainly at night and will run for their hiding places when they are exposed to light. This means you usually won't see them in the daytime. Even at night, it's hard to see them except in the few seconds it takes them to run away when you flip on a light. Since cockroaches come into our homes to eat food that is left on countertops and in open garbage, make sure you clean up after cooking and eating. Rinse out your recyclables, and seal your trash tightly. These **precautions** will help you get rid of any cockroaches that may be in your home.

Nothing we do will keep cockroaches away forever. After all, they have been around since before the dinosaurs! As well as eating what humans eat, cockroaches can eat anything organic. They will eat the glue off a postage stamp, paper, cloth, and even electrical wiring insulation. On the plus side, they clean the environment and help recycle garbage. Of the 4,000 species of cockroaches, less than 1% are a **nuisance** to human beings. Loud Madagascar hissing cockroaches are even kept as pets by many people. Whether you love them or hate them, they're here to stay.

Read each question. Circle the letter of the best answer.

1. What is a possible conclusion you could make based on the second paragraph?

   A A cockroach needs to eat to live.

   B A cockroach lives underground.

   C A cockroach can survive in extreme conditions.

   D A cockroach needs protection and food in extreme conditions.

2. What is the most important conclusion you can draw from the passage?

   A Cockroaches can survive without their heads for one week before they starve.

   B Cockroaches can hold their breath for 40 minutes.

   C Cockroaches can fit into very small cracks.

   D Cockroaches can live through conditions that most other living things would not survive.

3. Why do cockroaches live near people?

   A Cockroaches like the way humans smell.

   B Cockroaches eat the same things that people eat.

   C Everyone wants cockroaches to live near them.

   D Cockroaches cannot live without people.

4. Why is it difficult to step on a cockroach?

   A Cockroaches can see behind themselves.

   B Cockroaches can hear your footsteps.

   C Cockroaches can sense air moving as your foot comes down.

   D Cockroaches are flat.

5. In a home, you are most likely to find cockroaches —

   A on the ceilings

   B in the bedrooms

   C inside the windows

   D near the kitchen garbage

6. Why have cockroaches been around since before dinosaurs?

   A Cockroaches are hardy.

   B Cockroaches are scary.

   C Cockroaches are flat.

   D Cockroaches are blind.

7. One reason cockroaches are good to have is because they —

   A are like dinosaurs

   B help recycle garbage

   C do not eat food

   D come out during the day

8. On a separate sheet of paper, draw your own conclusion about why you think cockroaches will be around forever. Support your conclusion with details from the passage.

LADDERS to SUCCESS

LESSON 7

Interpreting Figurative Language

Before you begin this lesson, take this quiz to show what you know about figurative language. Read this story about walking in the rain. Then answer the questions.

NO THANKS, I'LL WALK

It had been a tough practice, and she was exhausted. She pulled her damp hair under her hat and put her headphones on. Then she jogged down the stairs to the Philadelphia subway. She squeezed into the car with everyone else, like ants in a tunnel. The subway jolted forward, and she nodded her head along with the beat coming through her headphones. She felt like she was floating along the rails.

She got off at her stop and jumped up the stairs. She could feel her leg muscles burning from the drills they had done at practice. She was just one short bus ride away from collapsing into bed.

A soft rain fell, and it made the air taste fresh, like spring. The bus was there, waiting, and she gazed upward into the bus's large windows. The light inside the bus was a sickly green. She saw passengers sitting inside the bus with **listless** stares. She turned her gaze from the bus to the sights around her. The lights of the city sparkled off the puddles and the wet sidewalks. The raindrops seemed to dance along with the music on her headphones.

She looked up at the bus once more, lifeless as a coffin. She turned and began to walk home in the rain.

Circle the letter of the best answer.

1. The people on the subway are compared to —

   A raindrops

   B ants in a tunnel

   C spring

   D a coffin

2. <u>Collapsing</u> into bed means —

   A jumping with excitement

   B getting in carefully

   C getting in reluctantly

   D falling suddenly

3. When the narrator says that the bus is like a coffin, she means that —

   A it is not moving

   B people around it are crying

   C it looks lifeless

   D it is made of wood

4. When the raindrops seem to dance, it means that they are —

   A very warm

   B lively

   C slow

   D large

Introduction

Authors use **figurative language** to make a comparison that creates a picture in a reader's mind.

To interpret figurative language,

- Look for one thing that is compared to another. You might notice the words *like* or *as*.
- Picture the two things in your mind. Think about how they are alike.
- Look for ways that the author exaggerates. Exaggerating means making things seem *more* than they really are.

Here's How

Read these sentences. How does the author use comparisons to help you form pictures in your mind?

"I was running a million miles an hour. Sweat was pouring down my face, and my lungs felt like they were on fire."

Think About It

1. The speaker uses the word *like* to compare the feeling in his lungs to being on fire.

2. Being on fire is painful. His lungs were not hot, but they were painful.

3. The speaker exaggerates when he says he was running "a million miles an hour." He is saying that he was running very quickly.

Try This Strategy

Monitor and Clarify

When you **monitor and clarify,** you check to make sure that you understand what you are reading.

- Pause after reading each section or paragraph and restate the main ideas.
- If you did not understand the main ideas, reread the section.
- As you reread each sentence, restate the ideas in ordinary, more simple language.

Read the story. Use the Reading Guide for tips. The tips will help you monitor and clarify and interpret figurative language as you read.

 Reading Guide

Travis compares the basement to a blanket. Think about qualities that both things share.

Make sure you understand the language Travis uses. See if you can use your own words to describe the same things.

Think about the words Travis uses. Decide which descriptions are exaggerations.

A WILD STORY

Travis walked ahead of the group, skipping backwards as he talked.

"The basement was completely black," he said. "It was like I had a blanket over my head."

"Sure, Travis," one of the other boys said. They were used to Travis's wild stories.

"I was running a million miles an hour. Sweat was pouring down my face, and my lungs were on fire. I was running, running, and this thing was coming up behind me. I could hear it growling like a bear. I was almost to the stairs, but this thing was right behind me."

Travis acted out the story, jogging in place.

"I got to the stairs, and I just barely made it up. I flew up like a rocket. But guess what?"

"What?" one of the boys finally said.

"The door at the top of the stairs wouldn't open," Travis said. The boys stopped walking.

"What happened?" one of them asked.

Travis grinned. "I turned the light on. And when I turned around, I nearly died. Standing in front of me was a wild wolf with dripping fangs."

"Yeah, right, Travis," one of the boys said.

Now use what you learned to interpret figurative language.

Answer the questions on the next page.

Practice interpreting figurative language in the story you just read.

EXAMPLE

Travis uses the image of being covered by a blanket to show that the basement was —

A warm

B soft

C dark

D frightening

Find the sentence where one thing is compared to another.

In the second paragraph, the basement's darkness is compared to being covered by a blanket.

Picture the two things in your mind. Think about how they might be similar.

Having a blanket over your head can be warm and dark. The basement is also dark. The author uses the image of being covered by a blanket to show how dark the basement is.

Now read each question. Circle the letter of the best answer.

1. Why did Travis compare himself to a rocket?

   A because he felt like he was on fire

   B to show how fast he moved

   C because he was turning red

   D because he was in space

2. When the thing growls like a bear, that tells us that it is —

   A fierce

   B large

   C furry

   D heavy

3. Saying that Travis nearly died when he turned around is probably —

   A an exaggeration

   B a mistake

   C a comparison

   D a true statement

4. Travis uses figurative language to make the story more —

   A funny

   B true

   C boring

   D exciting

Real-Life Batman Shares His Love of Bats

Bats are Merlin Tuttle's life work.

AUSTIN, TX—They call him Batman. While Merlin Tuttle may not be a superhero, he sure loves bats. Tuttle, president of Bat Conservation International, uses his organization to protect more than 1,100 species of bats worldwide.

Tuttle's organization also helps people overcome their fear of bats. The group teaches people all about these misunderstood mammals. "People are only afraid of what they don't understand," says Tuttle. "The more you know about a group of animals, the more you appreciate them, and the more interesting they become to you."

Tuttle first became interested in bats at the age of nine. He began studying them when he was 15. He founded Bat Conservation International in 1982.

One of the things Tuttle loves about bats is that the differences between them can be like night and day. "There are bats that are as cute as any puppy or kitten, and those that are as strange as E.T. or any dinosaur," Tuttle says. Bats also differ in size, color, and even the way they fly. Some bats fly like helicopters, while others fly like jets.

Write About It

Reread the last paragraph of the article. Fill in this graphic organizer to show how bats are described. Use two examples from the text.

Subject Being Compared	What It Is Compared to	How They Are Alike
bat		
bat		

Ladder to Success

Review

You have learned that authors sometimes use **figurative language** to create an image in the reader's mind. Figurative language might compare two things or exaggerate details.

Review the steps for interpreting figurative language.

- Look for two things that are compared in a description. The words *like* and *as* often signal a comparison.
- Picture the two things being compared, and imagine how they are alike.
- Look for places where the author exaggerates to describe an image more strongly.

Practice 1

Read the following passage. As you read, look for figurative language, including comparisons and exaggerations.

> When the break dancing craze exploded like a firecracker, break dancing fashion helped make it possible. The loose track suits allowed dancers to flop around like rag dolls. With the slick nylon, they could slide like snakes across the floor. Low sneakers were comfortable and gave the dancers a grip as they flew and spun. The boom box was like a musical suitcase that could be taken from place to place. When break dancing made it onto TV, people across the country followed its style.

In the first box of the chart below, list examples of figurative language. In the second box, write the actual meaning of the author's ideas.

Figurative Language	Meaning

Practice 2

Read the passage. As you read, think about how the comparisons help create an image of San Antonio.

San Antonio is the heart of Texas in almost every way. The city lies right near the center of the state, and it has a little bit of almost everything that makes Texas special. The spicy sound of Latin music mixes with the shuffle of country and western. The vibrant smells of Mexican food blend with the homey taste of southern cooking. Above it all, the Tower of the Americas stands like a lighthouse, welcoming people from all over to this friendly Texas city.

A visit to San Antonio can be like a trip back through time. The Spanish explorers left a little bit of their **architecture,** language, and history behind. The streets of El Mercado look like they lead right to Mexico. Walk into any barbecue joint, and you would expect to see a cowboy.

Use this graphic organizer to interpret figurative language.

Subject Being Compared	What It Is Compared to	How They Are Alike
	a heart	
	a lighthouse	

Practice 3

Read the passage. Then interpret figurative language to answer the questions. Make a graphic organizer on a separate sheet of paper to organize your thoughts.

It was gray and windy, and the pool was nearly empty. Luis didn't mind the weather, though. He put his goggles on and pressed them into his face until he could feel the suction on his skin, and then he dove.

Once he was underwater, sounds became echoes. He kicked furiously, feeling the water rush past him like a cool breeze. He burst through the surface like a dolphin. Sounds suddenly became high and sharp again. He sucked in a deep breath and plunged beneath the water.

He looked down at the familiar painted lines and waffle-shaped drains on the cement bottom. As he looked, he thought he saw something glimmering like a jewel against the blue background. He rose and took another breath before diving down.

The pressure punched him in the ears as he reached the bottom of the deep end. He grabbed the shining object and pulled it up with him. It was a man's thick gold watch. Water had leaked into the face, and the hands were dead. Luis looked around. No adults were near the pool. Who would jump into the water with this thing on his wrist?

1. What figurative language does the writer use to describe Luis swimming?

_____

_____

2. Picture the waffle-shaped drains and describe what they look like.

_____

_____

3. When the author says that the watch hands were "*dead,*" what does the author mean?

_____

_____

Introduction

Authors use **figurative language** to describe things in a colorful way. Figurative language may compare one thing to another or exaggerate details.

As you saw on pages 97–99, graphic organizers can help you interpret figurative language.

- Identify the figurative language and write it in the first box.
- In the second box, tell how the two objects being compared are alike.
- In the last box, write the meaning of the figurative language.

Here's How

Read these sentences. How do the comparisons help describe the girls?

The girls blew into the house like flower petals on the breeze. Cari looked especially happy. Her cheeks were glowing as if it were cold outside, but the day was warm.

Think About It

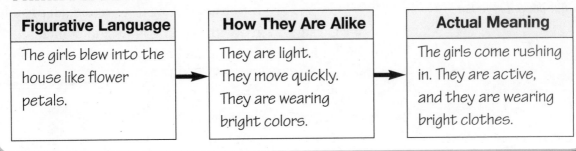

Figurative Language	How They Are Alike	Actual Meaning
The girls blew into the house like flower petals.	They are light. They move quickly. They are wearing bright colors.	The girls come rushing in. They are active, and they are wearing bright clothes.

Try This Strategy

Access Prior Knowledge

When you **access prior knowledge,** you use what you already know about a topic or a situation to help understand a similar situation or something new.

- Before reading, skim the passage to get an idea about the topic.
- Think of what you already know about that topic or subject.
- If you come to unfamiliar language, review your knowledge of the topic and see if you can relate it to the new meanings of the words.

Read the story. Use the Reading Guide for tips that can help you access prior knowledge and interpret figurative language as you read.

Reading Guide

What phrases can you find that are exaggerations?

Can you picture a boiling tea kettle? How is this like the girls?

Have you ever used the phrase "like a baby"? What does this mean?

Notice the clue word as. *What comparisons does it signal?*

Painting Cari

The girls blew into the house like flower petals on the breeze. Cari looked especially happy. Her cheeks were glowing as if it were cold outside, but the day was warm. Leyla ran to her older sister and gave her a big hug. Cari squeezed as though she would never let go.

"I missed you so much!" she said. Cari's wedding had been the day before. Today, she was spending one more morning at home before leaving with her new husband. They would take part in a tradition her husband's family had brought from Turkey. They would paint Cari's hands with beautiful henna designs. Her friends were here to help. They bubbled over with excitement like boiling tea kettles.

"Come help with the henna, Leyla!" Cari called. Leyla stepped quietly between the older girls. She felt like a baby with all the young women around.

"Use the brush to paint a design," Cari said. Her hands were already covered with twirling vines and pointed shapes, like the wall of a mosque. Leyla picked up a brush and sat near Cari's arm. She had never lived in a house without her sister before. She would even miss the way she looked— bright as the sun, fresh as the lilies in the backyard garden.

That's what she would paint on Cari's arm: a lily. Then Cari could bring a piece of their home into her new house.

Answer the questions on the next page.

Practice identifying figurative language by answering questions about the story you just read. Read each question. Circle the letter of the best answer.

1. Why does the author use the image of lilies to describe Cari?

   A because she dresses in white

   B because she looks fresh

   C because she smells nice

   D because she is bright

2. The author compares Leyla and her friends to a boiling tea kettle to show that they are —

   A creative

   B thirsty

   C nervous

   D excited

3. Which phrase is an exaggeration?

   A squeezed as though she would never let go

   B hands were already covered with twirling vines

   C spending one more morning at home

   D like flower petals on the breeze

4. Leyla feels like a baby because —

   A the other girls are older

   B she is playing with toys

   C she doesn't know how to hold a brush

   D she is crying

5. A mosque is probably —

   A painted with henna

   B plain

   C covered with designs

   D boring

6. On a separate sheet of paper, explain why Leyla thinks Cari is "bright as the sun."

The Georgia Aquarium was built to look like a cruise ship.

World's Largest Aquarium Opens in Georgia

ATLANTA, GA—Step inside Atlanta's newest attraction, and you'll feel like you have **descended** to the ocean floor. More than 100,000 animals surround you in over 8 million gallons of water. Sharks, whales, penguins, starfish, and other sea creatures move past like a parade, and tropical fish light up the tanks like a fireworks display. The world's largest aquarium is truly a sight to behold.

The Georgia Aquarium may also be the world's most unique museum. A trip through the many display tanks is like watching a symphony of light and sound. These tanks feature music, spotlights, and computer-generated images.

In addition to display tanks, the aquarium is home to a banquet hall that can seat more than 1,000 people. The aquarium also features a "4-D" movie theater that uses special effects to teach viewers about sea creatures from around the world.

What's inside is not the only unique thing at the Georgia Aquarium. The building itself is shaped like a cruise ship, forging through the downtown area. The aquarium is well on its way to becoming one of Atlanta's main tourist attractions. It is expected to receive up to 2 million visitors in its first year.

Write About It

Select one subject from the article that is compared to another using figurative language. In a sentence, tell how the two things being compared are alike. Write another sentence describing the thing in another way, using your own figurative language.

Read this article about a new museum in Washington, D.C. Then answer the questions on the next page.

I Spy !

You walk into a building that looks about as exciting as a slice of bread. The dull shell of the building, however, is like a false mustache disguising a secret agent. A man tells you to think of a fake name for yourself. He tells you to think of a fake birthday and a fake hometown. This isn't a walk through some stuffy art museum. This is the International Spy Museum, and you are now on a mission.

The spy museum is the only museum dedicated to the art of lying, sneaking around, and telling secrets. The mood of the place is as eerie as a haunted house. The exhibits are slick and modern, with displays of gadgets and spy equipment. Here you'll find tiny cameras and microphones no bigger than a bird's eye. You'll find **transmitters** stuffed inside ordinary-looking shoes and a gun disguised as a tube of lipstick. You may even see a spy changing into a complete disguise like a chameleon changing colors. If you like secrets, you'll be in paradise.

The guides might pull you aside and teach you the tricks of the trade. You'll learn how to spot a government agent stalking you like a tiger. You'll be able to look for an escape out of a tight squeeze. And speaking of squeezes, you might like to crawl on your belly through the ducts of the building and listen to the conversations taking place below. Signs at the beginning of the museum warn you that you might be watched at any time. Walking through this museum, you'll feel like you're under a microscope.

Remember that fake name, birthday, and hometown you gave as you entered? You'd better remember them, because there's a test at the end. A museum worker quizzes you on your fake identity. Can you pass the test, or will you break down and show your true colors? Find out if you have what it takes to become a real-life James Bond.

Read each question. Circle the letter of the best answer.

1. How is the building like a fake mustache?

   A It is furry.

   B It is funny looking.

   C It is small.

   D It is a disguise.

2. The building is compared to a slice of bread because —

   A it is shaped like a rectangle

   B it is flat

   C it does not look interesting

   D it looks like a bakery

3. A camera is like a bird's eye because it —

   A is small

   B sees for great distances

   C is surrounded by feathers

   D looks pretty

4. The spy is compared to a chameleon because he is —

   A completely disguised

   B like a horror movie

   C moving quickly

   D hard to see

5. A government agent stalks you —

   A slowly and steadily

   B silently and fiercely

   C obviously

   D loudly

6. Visitors to the spy museum feel as if they are under a microscope because —

   A the museum is full of science

   B they feel very small

   C they feel as if they are being watched

   D they are looking at spy equipment

7. The author says "you'll be in paradise" to show that the spy museum —

   A will be enjoyable to anyone

   B will be enjoyable to people who like secrets

   C has everything you will ever want

   D is very beautiful

8. On a separate sheet of paper, explain the meaning of the phrase "a tight squeeze."

Show What You Know

Before you begin this lesson, take this quiz to show what you know about fact and opinion. Read this passage about music recording. Then answer the questions that follow.

The Music Revolution

I sure am glad I wasn't a kid in 1877. That was the year Thomas Edison invented the phonograph. It was a little machine that recorded sounds by scratching a piece of thick tinfoil. The recording sounded scratchy and rough. It had an annoying **metallic** sound. My favorite music would have sounded terrible.

Things got a bit better when records were invented. Records had a pretty good sound quality. But you could easily scratch or break them. Plus, it's hard to carry around a record that is a foot wide!

The next big breakthrough in music recording was the audiotape. An audiotape was small and easy to store. You could also record music onto a blank tape. However, the sound quality was still not perfect.

Finally came CDs and MP3s. CDs are disks that store music in a digital form. In a CD player, a laser reads tiny pits on a CD. The sound quality is great. Best of all, you can quickly skip from one song to another. MP3s are even better. They are bits of digital information stored right on a computer chip. Thousands of MP3s can fit in the palm of your hand. That sure beats carrying around a bulky record or a phonograph!

Circle the letter of the best answer.

1. Which statement tells how the writer feels?

   A Edison invented the phonograph.
   B Records could be easily scratched.
   C The sound quality was not good.
   D Many MP3s can fit in your hand.

2. One fact from the passage is —

   A a CD player uses a laser
   B an audiotape is better than a record
   C records have good sound quality
   D MP3s are better than CDs

3. Which word in the first paragraph helps to tell how the writer feels?

   A recording
   B scratching
   C invented
   D terrible

4. How does the writer feel about MP3s?

   A The writer thinks they are not as good as CDs.
   B The writer thinks they are annoying.
   C The writer doesn't care about them.
   D The writer thinks they are great.

Introduction

A **fact** is a statement that can be proved true or false. An **opinion** is a statement that tells how someone thinks or feels. In fiction, a fact is something that happens or is true in the story, while an opinion is what a character thinks or feels.

To distinguish between fact and opinion,

- Decide if the statement tells you something that can be checked, or if it is true in the story. This is probably a fact.

- Look for words that might show an opinion, such as *I think, I feel,* or *should.* Also look for describing words that show feelings, such as *great, best, awful,* or *wrong.* In fiction, look for ways that a character tells how he or she feels.

Here's How

Read this paragraph. Can you find one fact and one opinion?

Many history books tell how the Dutch bought Manhattan from the Native Americans. They exchanged 24 dollars worth of beads and other items for the island. That seems like quite the bargain.

Think About It

1. The first sentence includes a number and a source for the information. You could go to a history book and check this fact.

2. The second statement has the words *seems* and *bargain,* which tell how the author feels. It is an opinion.

Try This Strategy

Access Prior Knowledge

When you **access prior knowledge,** you review what you already know.

- Read the title and look at the picture to see what the passage is about. Think about what you already know about the topic or situation.

- As you read, think about what you know about the facts and ideas.

- Think of anything else you have seen, heard, or experienced, such as stories, movies, or real-life events that remind you of the passage.

Read the article. Use the Reading Guide for tips. The tips will help you access prior knowledge and distinguish between fact and opinion as you read.

 Reading Guide

Read the title. Think of what you know about Manhattan. (Manhattan is part of New York City.) Today it would be very expensive to buy.

Look for words that show how the author feels.

Think of what you know about the Native Americans and the settlers. Use what you know to help you distinguish the facts and opinions.

Buying Manhattan

Many history books tell how the Dutch bought Manhattan from the Native Americans. They exchanged 24 dollars worth of beads and other items for the island. That seems like quite the bargain. However, there is more to the story than those history books tell us. The tribe that sold the land was not as foolish as some people think.

The Native Americans and Europeans had different ideas about buying land than we do today. Native American tribes usually didn't buy land from each other because land was **abundant.** Even in Europe, land sales simply gave the buyers the right to farm and develop the land. Native Americans continued to use the island for hunting and fishing.

As it turns out, the settlers didn't even buy the land from the correct people. They bought it from a tribe that traded on the island, but lived miles away. The Dutch had to pay other Indian tribes over and over again. In the end, the Dutch were the ones who wound up looking silly in this **transaction.**

Now use what you learned to distinguish between fact and opinion.

Answer the questions on the next page.

Practice the Skill 1

Practice distinguishing between fact and opinion in the article you just read.

EXAMPLE

The statement "They bought it from a tribe that traded on the island" is —

A probably false

B an opinion

C a fact that can be checked

D how the author feels

Look for clues that the statement might be a fact.

It tells about an action that happened, so it can be checked.

Check for any opinion clue words or words that show how the writer feels.

The statement doesn't have any opinion clue words such as I think. Therefore, it is a fact.

Now read each question. Circle the letter of the best answer.

1. One fact from the passage is —

   A 24 dollars is quite the bargain

   B the Europeans bought the land from the wrong people

   C there is more to the story than the history books tell us

   D the Dutch were the ones who wound up looking silly

2. One term that gives you a clue to the author's opinion is —

   A different

   B foolish

   C bought

   D Native Americans

3. One opinion the author has about the Native Americans is —

   A they were still able to use the land

   B they were the ones who wound up looking silly

   C they were not as foolish as some people think

   D they usually didn't buy land from each other

4. Which words would most likely come before an opinion?

   A as it turns out

   B in the end

   C many history books tell

   D that seems like

COMPANY SHUT DOWN FOR SELLING LAND ON MOON

Lunar Embassy to China sold land on the moon for $37 an acre.

BEIJING, CHINA—It seems that some people will believe anything. A Chinese company, called Lunar Embassy to China, has had its license taken away after selling land on the moon for about 37 dollars an acre. Apparently, the problem of actually getting to the moon did not bother investors. Thirty-four investors had bought 49 acres of moon property before the company was shut down.

The Chinese government ruled that selling land on the moon was a form of fraud, and therefore illegal. One government official said that selling land on the moon was "nothing but a beautiful dream." Lunar Embassy chief Li Jie was unhappy with the decision. Jie believes there is nothing wrong with selling land on the moon and that his company's license should be returned.

According to the company, each landowner received a deed to the land, along with the right to dig for minerals for up to two miles. The Chinese government has asked Lunar Embassy to return the money to investors.

Write About It

Now practice the skill using a real news story. Complete this graphic organizer by telling which statements are facts and which are opinions.

Facts	
Opinions	

Ladder to Success

Review

You have learned how to **distinguish between fact and opinion.** A fact is a statement that can be proved true or false. An opinion tells how the author thinks or feels.

Review the steps you can use to distinguish between fact and opinion.

- Look for clues that a statement is a fact, such as numbers or sources. A fact can be checked and proved true or false.

- Look for clues that a statement is an opinion, such as strong words or clue words such as *I believe.* In fiction, look for statements of what a character feels or believes.

Practice 1

Read the following passage. As you read, look for clues to distinguish fact from opinion. Look for ideas or events that could be checked. Look for words that signal the character's opinion.

"I was terrible," said Bryson. He and Dad rode home from the soccer game.

"How could you say that?" Dad asked. "You scored a goal, and you took the ball from the other team twice. I thought you were great."

Bryson sighed. "But I lost the ball once. And then when I was chasing one of the other guys, I tripped and fell. I looked stupid."

"I guess it's all how you look at it," Dad said. "I was proud. And I'm pretty sure you deserve an ice cream."

Use the chart below to separate facts and opinions.

Fact	Opinion

Practice 2

Read the passage. Look for facts and opinions in the text.

We are very sorry to report that Mrs. Weaver, our fifth-grade teacher, will be leaving at the end of the year. Mrs. Weaver has been teaching at Hoover Elementary for almost 25 years, and she is one of our finest teachers. During that time, she has brought up fifth-grade reading test scores by 40 percent. She has brightened our days with her warm smile and hilarious stories.

The good news is that Mrs. Weaver is going on an adventure. She'll be flying to Antarctica, where she plans to spend the winter at a research station. Antarctica is the coldest place on Earth. We think she'll do fine there, and the researchers will love her just as much as we do. Let's wish her luck!

Use this graphic organizer to identify opinions from the passage. Write the opinions in the left column. Write words that signal that the statement is an opinion in the right column.

Opinions	Opinion Clue Words

Practice 3

Read the passage. Then distinguish between fact and opinion to answer the questions. Make a graphic organizer on a separate sheet of paper to organize your thoughts.

You may have heard of the Great Chicago Fire. You probably haven't heard of the Peshtigo Fire, but you should have. It tore through Peshtigo, Wisconsin, destroying more land and killing more people than the Chicago fire.

Why haven't you heard of it? Because it occurred on the same day as the Chicago Fire. The Chicago Fire was more exciting because it was in the heart of a city. Journalists and rescuers could get there easily. It left the much deadlier Peshtigo Fire virtually unknown.

The Peshtigo Fire is one of the most horrible natural disasters in U.S. history. Like the Chicago Fire, it was fueled by extremely dry weather. Peshtigo was a lumber community, so piles of dry wood were everywhere. Winds spread the fire quickly. As the firestorm grew, it created tornadoes of flame that picked up railroad cars like toys.

No one knows how many people died in the Peshtigo Fire. Some towns were so completely destroyed that no population records were left and no one was around to remember who had lived there. The Peshtigo Fire deserves to be as famous as the Chicago Fire, if not more famous.

1. How does the author feel about the Peshtigo Fire?

_____

_____

2. What are two statements in the essay that are facts?

_____

_____

3. What are two statements in the essay that are opinions? How can you tell?

_____

_____

Guided Instruction 2

Introduction

A **fact** is a statement that can be proved true or false. An **opinion** is a statement that tells how an author feels or thinks. In fiction, a fact is something that happened or is true in the story, while an opinion is what a character thinks or feels.

As you saw on pages 111–113, graphic organizers can help you distinguish between fact and opinion.

- Create a web with facts and opinions.
- Under **Facts,** write ideas that can be checked or that happened in the story.
- Under **Opinions,** write ideas that include what someone thinks or feels.

Here's How

Read these sentences. Which ideas are facts about BMX, and which are opinions?

Racing is one of the two major forms of BMX. The athletes race around a dirt track, often sailing over jumps and bumps as they go. It can get your heart pumping whether you're a racer or just a spectator.

Think About It

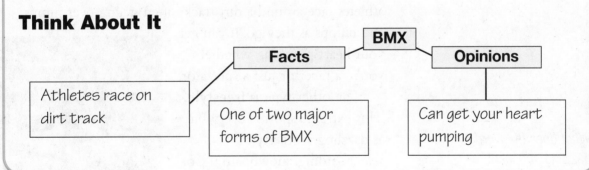

Try This Strategy

Scan and Skim

When you **scan and skim,** you look over a passage to see what it's about.

- Read the title and look at any pictures. What is the passage about?
- Scan the passage. If the passage includes dialogue and characters, it is probably fiction. If it contains lots of facts, it is probably nonfiction.
- Skim the passage to find important words. Think about these words as you predict what you will read about.

Read the article. Use the Reading Guide for tips that can help you scan and skim and distinguish fact from opinion as you read.

 Reading Guide

Scan and skim the passage to see what it is about. Does it include facts? What do you think they will tell about?

Which describing word tells how the author feels about BMX?

Skim the text for clue words. Which words stand out as opinion words?

What does the word dazzling *suggest?*

BiKiNG WiTH STyLE

The riders fly around the dirt track. They kick up specks of mud and debris as they go. In another part of the arena, kids on bikes soar over ramps. They flip up and down half-pipes, doing 360s and standing on their handlebars. This is the sport of BMX, one of the most exciting extreme sports.

BMX stands for bicycle motocross. Motocross was originally a motorcycle sport. But mountain bikers and kids who just liked doing tricks on their bikes soon made the sport their own. These cool **innovators** were the first to put knobby tires on their short wheels and take their bikes into the dirt. Soon, the sport caught on. Now, you can buy special bikes just for BMX.

Racing is one of the two major forms of BMX. The athletes race around a dirt track, often sailing over jumps and bumps as they go. It can get your heart pumping whether you're a racer or just a spectator.

The other type is **freestyle.** This extreme sport is every bit as dazzling as freestyle skateboarding, snowboarding, or motocross. The bicyclists throw themselves over high jumps, doing twists and flips as they go. It's not easy to do, but it's a thrill to watch.

Answer the questions on the next page.

Practice the Skill 2

Practice distinguishing between fact and opinion by answering questions about the article you just read. Read each question. Circle the letter of the best answer.

1. The facts in this article —

   A   tell what it's like to watch BMX

   B   tell how BMX racers feel

   C   describe the sport of BMX

   D   tell how much the author likes BMX

2. Which statement is a fact?

   A   There are two major forms of BMX.

   B   BMX is one of the most exciting sports.

   C   The people who changed their bikes were cool innovators.

   D   It will get your heart pumping.

3. An example of an opinion from this passage is —

   A   BMX started as a motorcycle sport

   B   freestyle involves doing tricks

   C   it's a thrill to watch

   D   you can buy BMX bikes

4. Which word from the passage signals an opinion?

   A   cool

   B   soar

   C   major

   D   freestyle

5. Which statement is a fact about freestyle BMX?

   A   It is every bit as dazzling as freestyle skateboarding.

   B   BMX is the most exciting extreme sport.

   C   The athletes race around a dirt track.

   D   The bicyclists are very daring.

6. On a separate sheet of paper, rewrite one paragraph of the passage, telling only facts and leaving out the opinions.

NEWS FLASH!

Students Relive Lewis and Clark's Journey

A group of young bikers followed the path of Lewis and Clark.

MONTICELLO, VA—A daring group of students and teachers have pedaled their way across 5,000 miles of American history. The group call themselves the "Corps of ReDiscovery." They biked along the same path traveled by Meriwether Lewis and William Clark when they explored the Louisiana Territory over 200 years ago. The group began their journey at Monticello, President Thomas Jefferson's home in Virginia. The purchase of the Louisiana Territory from France was Jefferson's idea, as was the Lewis and Clark **expedition.**

During their trip, the group faced 100-degree heat and 45-mile-per-hour winds. Each day, they rode for ten hours. "At first it was hard," said Roxy Kurta, a thirteen-year-old girl who was part of the group. As they progressed all the way to the Pacific Ocean, they found it easier.

The entire group learned how difficult a trip it must have been for Lewis and Clark. While this group had detailed maps, Lewis and Clark were in **uncharted** territory. They could not be certain they were headed in the right direction.

The journey was not easy for these students, but it was a valuable experience, they said. "I think I've learned about America," said thirteen-year-old Lincoln Pitcher.

Write About It

How would you like to travel with these students on the Corps of ReDiscovery? Write what you think the experience would be like, using at least one fact and one opinion.

Show What You Learned

LADDERS
to SUCCESS

LESSON
8
Distinguishing
Between Fact
and Opinion

Read this essay about Chinatown. Then answer the questions on the next page.

Chinatown, U.S.A.

If you've been to a large city, chances are you've been near a Chinatown. There are Chinatowns in New York City, San Francisco, Houston, Chicago, and Philadelphia. There were once Chinatowns in Pittsburgh and Newark, New Jersey. Chinatowns can be found in cities around the world, such as London, Paris, and Tokyo. They are fascinating places to visit.

Chinatown is a neighborhood with a large population of Chinese people. The Chinese language is spoken by many residents, and Chinese symbols appear on signs, menus, and advertisements. You can buy delicious Chinese food and groceries, and you can find colorful Chinese clothing, toys, and decorations. Many Chinatowns are centers for Chinese culture. The residents celebrate holidays such as Chinese New Year, which is a thrilling celebration with fireworks, parades, and parties. You can find unique foods and products that are available nowhere else.

Why do so many cities have Chinatowns? Part of the reason is that Chinese immigrants want to create a comfortable place for themselves in a new country. Suppose one family moves from China to Pittsburgh. They do not speak very much English, and the food, culture, and stores are all unfamiliar. If they run into another family from China, they might decide to live near them. As more and more families arrive, the neighborhood soon becomes a center for Chinese immigrants. Some immigrants may open stores offering familiar foods and goods. The neighborhood becomes a welcoming and familiar sanctuary.

Unfortunately, prejudice has also played a role in creating Chinatowns. In many cities, people from China were once restricted to certain areas. Despite these difficulties, Chinese immigrants made Chinatown an exciting and unique neighborhood.

Today, Chinatown is not only for people of Chinese ancestry. People from all walks of life come to Chinatown to enjoy the delicious cuisine, colorful festivals, and unique shops. Next time you're near Chinatown, step inside and see a little bit of Chinese culture, right in your own city.

Read each question. Circle the letter of the best answer.

1. One fact about Chinatown is —

   A it's vibrant

   B the food is delicious

   C it's a fun place to visit

   D there is one in Philadelphia

2. One opinion about Chinatown is —

   A there is one in Paris

   B the celebrations are thrilling

   C you can buy Chinese products there

   D the Chinese language is spoken by many people

3. One word that tells you the second sentence in the last paragraph might be an opinion is —

   A cuisine

   B delicious

   C Chinatown

   D festivals

4. One fact that might be added to this passage is —

   A Chinatown is a great place to visit

   B Chinatown is often the most colorful part of a city

   C one of the largest Chinatowns is in San Francisco

   D the best time to visit Chinatown is during Chinese New Year

5. The author's statement that the shops are unique is —

   A an opinion

   B an exaggeration

   C a fact

   D false

6. Which is a fact about why Chinatowns exist?

   A Chinese is spoken by many residents in Chinatown.

   B Immigrants made Chinatown a pleasant neighborhood.

   C In many cities, people from China were restricted to certain areas.

   D People from all walks of life come to enjoy the delicious cuisine.

7. The first paragraph tells you —

   A an opinion about Chinatown

   B facts about Chinatown

   C facts and opinions about Chinatown

   D how the author feels about Chinatown

8. Rewrite the second sentence of the last paragraph, using only facts and no opinions.

120

Show What You Know

Before you begin this lesson, take this quiz to show what you know about author's purpose. First, read this article about urban legends. Then answer the questions that follow.

MODERN MYTHS

Has anyone ever told you that if you swallow your chewing gum, it stays in your stomach for seven years? Have you ever heard that Coca-Cola would be green if the brown syrup coloring were removed? Has a friend ever told you to look closely at the background of a movie to see a ghost? These stories are all strange. There is something else you should know: they aren't true.

False stories like these are called *urban legends.* Urban legends are stories passed on from person to person. The stories are often believed to be true. They start as jokes, misunderstandings, or even made-up stories. People pass them on as warnings, funny stories, and scary tales. The legend often starts with the phrase, "This happened to a friend of a friend."

The next time you hear a strange story, think carefully. Did anyone actually see this happen? If it is a "friend of a friend," it is probably a **myth.** Does the story have specific names, dates, and places you could check out? And finally, does the story really make sense?

Circle the letter of the best answer.

1. The writer wrote this article mainly to —

   A make you laugh

   B convince you to believe in urban legends

   C tell you what an urban legend is

   D share legends the writer believes

2. The article mainly —

   A tries to convince readers of something

   B gives information about something

   C tells an enjoyable story

   D describes a person, place, or thing

3. What message is the author sending?

   A Urban legends are false stories.

   B You shouldn't drink Coca-Cola.

   C Believe everything you hear.

   D Urban legends are not myths.

4. Why does the author ask the questions in the first paragraph?

   A to get information from the reader

   B to point out unanswered questions

   C to show that myths have existed for many years

   D to give examples of urban legends

Introduction

The **author's purpose** is the reason why an author writes a story or article. An author may write to entertain you or convince you of something. The author may also write to inform, or to give facts and details about a topic.

To determine author's purpose,

- Find out what the passage is mostly about.
- Ask yourself, "Is the passage written in a funny or entertaining way? Does it include opinion words or convincing ideas?"
- Think about whether the author gives lots of facts about a topic.
- Decide whether the author's purpose is to entertain, persuade, or inform.

Here's How

Read these sentences. What is the author's purpose for this paragraph?

It had been a long week. Between studying for three tests and going to basketball tryouts at night, I was going non-stop. Then I had to baby-sit Thursday night. By Friday, I could barely keep my eyes open!

Think About It

1. The passage is mostly about a character who is exhausted.

2. The phrase "I could barely keep my eyes open!" is written in a funny way.

3. The paragraph does not give lots facts about a topic.

4. The author's purpose is to entertain.

Try This Strategy

Predict

When you **predict,** you try to think of what a passage will be about or what will happen next.

- Read the title and look at any illustrations to get an idea of the topic.
- As you read, pause after each paragraph and predict what will happen next.
- Check your predictions at the end to see if you were correct.

Read the story. Use the Reading Guide for tips. The tips will help you predict and determine the author's purpose as you read.

 Reading Guide

THREE-POINTER

The title sounds like the story will be about basketball, but the first paragraph is about being overtired.

It had been a long week. Between studying for three tests and going to basketball tryouts at night, I was going non-stop. Then I had to baby-sit Thursday night. By Friday, I could barely keep my eyes open!

At lunch, I was the last one to the table. All the chairs were already filled.

"Pull up a seat," said Lucille. I grabbed a chair from another table and squeezed my tray in with all the others. There wasn't much room, so my tray hung off the end of the table.

The author is setting up a situation that looks bad for the narrator. Make a prediction about what will happen next.

I'm not sure how I fell asleep with all the noise in the lunchroom. As I nodded off, my hand slammed the edge of my tray. The tray flipped over, sending spaghetti all over me. I reached out to save my dinner roll. Instead of catching the roll, I slapped it. It flew toward the floor, hitting my fork along the way at just the right angle. The fork flew upwards, sailed over everyone's head, and swished into the garbage can.

The sudden, messy action might remind you of a funny movie. The author is telling a funny story.

"Three points!" shouted Lucille, and the whole room suddenly cheered.

Now use what you learned to determine the author's purpose.

Answer the questions on the next page.

Practice the Skill 1

Practice determining the author's purpose of the story you just read.

EXAMPLE

The main event in this story is —

A funny

B sad

C informative

D convincing

Think of what the passage is about.

The passage is about a girl who falls asleep and makes a mess in the cafeteria.

Look for words and ideas that entertain, persuade, or give facts about a topic.

The main event in the story is funny and entertaining.

Decide the author's purpose.

The author's purpose is to entertain, because the main event in the story is funny.

Now read each question. Circle the letter of the best answer.

1. This passage would best be described as —

   A a description of cafeterias

   B an informative article about student life

   C a fun story

   D an argument

2. What words best describe the passage?

   A serious and formal

   B casual and lighthearted

   C worried and concerned

   D angry and aggressive

3. Why does the author describe what happens to the fork?

   A to inform the reader about silverware

   B to explain what can happen to a fork when it is hit with a roll

   C to persuade the reader never to try this stunt

   D to make the reader laugh

4. What is the author's purpose in writing this passage?

   A to explain something

   B to tell an entertaining story

   C to convince the reader of something

   D to inform the reader of an issue

NEWS FLASH!

Woman Sets Sailing Record

MacArthur faced tough winds and stormy skies on her way to setting the sailing record.

ENGLAND—British sailor Ellen MacArthur has set a world record after sailing around the world in just 71 days. She is the fastest person to complete the trip by herself.

Sailing around the world with no one else aboard was not an easy task for the 28-year-old. MacArthur had to live on freeze-dried meals. She could sleep for only 15 to 30 minutes at a time. She also had to deal with harsh winds, icebergs, and technical problems with the boat. At one point during the difficult trip, MacArthur's 75-foot boat nearly collided with a whale!

MacArthur was greeted by 8,000 screaming fans as she sailed across the finish line in the harbor of her homeland, England. "It has been an unbelievable journey," she said afterward. "When I crossed the line I felt like collapsing on the floor and just falling asleep. I was absolutely over the moon."

From the sounds of it, MacArthur still has plenty of sailing left to do. "There are lots of records out there," she said. "I do not want to stop sailing this boat."

Write About It

Now you will practice the skill using a real news article. Complete this graphic organizer by filling in clues from the article that support the author's purpose.

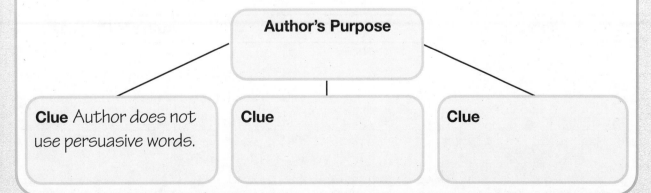

Author's Purpose

Clue Author does not use persuasive words.

Clue

Clue

LESSON

9

Determining Author's Purpose

Review

You are learning how to **determine the author's purpose.** The author's purpose is the reason the author wrote a passage. The purpose could be to inform, to persuade, or to entertain.

Review the steps you can use to determine the author's purpose.

- Think about what the passage is mainly about.
- Look for words and phrases that are entertaining or persuasive.
- Look for facts and details that inform or describe.
- Decide if the author has written to entertain you, to persuade you, or to give information about a topic.

Practice 1

Read the following passage. As you read, think about the author's purpose. Decide what message the author is trying to send. Is the author's purpose to inform, persuade, or entertain?

> People who are glassblowers have quite a talent. Glassblowing is the art of shaping glass. A glassblower begins by heating a lump of glass until it becomes flexible. When glass is heated, it turns soft and stretchy, like **taffy.** The glassblower then places a gob of hot glass on the end of a long, hollow metal tube.
>
> When the glassblower blows into the tube, a bubble forms in the gob of glass. Then the metal tube is turned, and the glass twirls into new shapes. Different tools are used to yank and stretch the glass. An assortment of colors can also be drizzled onto the creation to make a truly unique design.

Fill in the boxes below. First, write the topic of the passage. Then write words and phrases that give clues about the author's purpose. In the last box, describe the author's purpose.

Topic	Clues	Author's Purpose

Practice 2

Read the passage. What is the author's purpose in writing?

My aunt and I sure do make great travel companions. Touring Italy together last spring was so much fun. We spent an entire week together, and we laughed the whole time!

When we first arrived in Rome, the capital of Italy, we were both exhausted because of the time change. We checked into our hotel and took a brief nap. Then we felt refreshed enough to explore the beautiful city. Rome has so much history. We saw ancient statues that have been around since 100 A.D. and earlier!

The Colosseum is one of the most famous landmarks in Rome. It was an **amphitheater** many years ago. Bullfights and other types of battles took place there. Today, it is half-fallen down and is there only for visitors to admire.

Another place we visited was the Spanish Steps. The Steps are a place for people to relax and **linger** during the midday. Italians like to take a long lunch. The Spanish Steps is where they meet with friends to eat and chill out.

My favorite stop was the local market. In this area of Rome, local merchants lined the streets. They sold fresh tomatoes, cucumbers, pizza, cheeses, and all sorts of fruit. Everything was delicious to eat, especially the gelato, which is Italian ice cream.

Italy certainly has a special beauty to it. I could spend a month there!

Use this graphic organizer to determine the author's purpose.

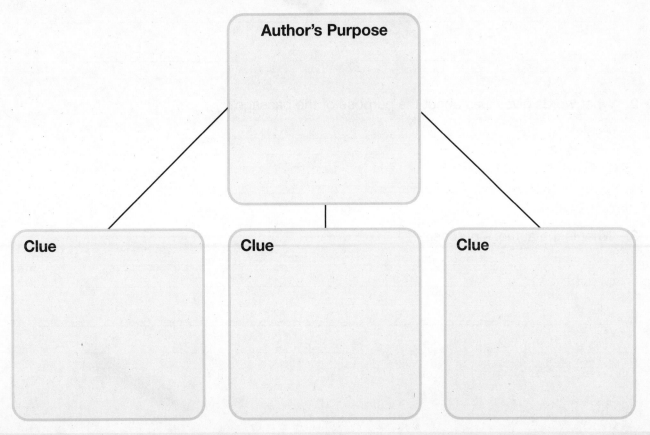

Practice 3

Read the passage. Then answer the questions to determine the author's purpose. Make a graphic organizer on a separate sheet of paper to organize your thoughts.

Dear Editor:

Now that I'm in fifth grade, I've decided that English is a crazy language. Some words just don't make sense at all! I mean, how can a *slim chance* and a *fat chance* mean the same thing? However, a *wise man* and a *wise guy* are opposites. If vegetarians eat vegetables, what do humanitarians eat? I think we should try to change a few of these wacky words.

The word "building," for example, should have a new name. Why is it called a "building" if it has already been built? People should call it a "built" from now on. "Apartment" is an unusual word, too. An "apartment" is joined, not apart. It's also a type of **complex,** so I've created the word "joinplex," which I believe is much more fitting.

I hope you agree with my suggestions. Once everyone knows about these new words, people will have an easier time learning the English language.

Yours truly,
Peter Crowley

1. What is the main idea or event of the passage?

   _____

   _____

2. What words give clues about the purpose of the passage?

   _____

   _____

3. What is the author's purpose?

   _____

   _____

Introduction

An author writes a passage to inform, persuade, or entertain. You can use the main idea of a passage to **determine the author's purpose.**

As you saw on pages 125–127, graphic organizers can help you determine the author's purpose.

- Write what the passage is about in the first box.
- In the second box, write words and phrases that entertain, persuade, or inform.
- In the third box, write the author's purpose.

Here's How

Read these sentences. What is the author's purpose for writing this paragraph?

America is actually named after a European explorer, Amerigo Vespucci. Vespucci was from Italy, just like Columbus. He sailed to America a few years after Columbus's first voyage. Unlike Columbus, however, Vespucci had a **hunch** that the land he was sailing to was new, unexplored land for the Europeans.

Think About It

Topic	Clues	Author's Purpose
Amerigo Vespucci	No entertaining words No persuasive words Facts and details: Vespucci from Italy; sailed a few years after Columbus	To inform the reader about Amerigo Vespucci

Try This Strategy

Summarize

When you **summarize,** you check your understanding by restating what you read in your own words.

- After you read each paragraph, think about the important ideas and state them in your own words.
- If you have trouble restating the important ideas, go back and reread the section.
- Once you have finished reading, summarize the main ideas of the passage.

Read the article. Use the Reading Guide for tips that can help you summarize and determine the author's purpose as you read.

 Reading Guide

After reading the first paragraph, what do you know about this passage?

What important facts do you read in the middle paragraphs? Why do you think the author included them?

Summarize what you read in your own words. What do you think the author's purpose was for writing this passage?

Naming America

Most people have heard that Christopher Columbus was the first European explorer to reach America. He **initiated** trade across the ocean between the Old World and the New World. We even celebrate Columbus Day in his honor. There is no doubt that Columbus is an important man in U.S. history.

Why isn't the land Columbus explored named after him? America is actually named after a European explorer, Amerigo Vespucci. Vespucci was from Italy, just like Columbus. He sailed to America a few years after Columbus's first voyage. Unlike Columbus, however, Vespucci had a **hunch** that the land he was sailing to was new, unexplored land for the Europeans. Columbus believed that he had landed in the East Indies and in Japan, places that were already well known.

When Vespucci came back from his travels, he spoke of beautiful land and great opportunity. His stories were published in newspapers across Europe. People enjoyed reading about his adventures and became excited about the New World that had been discovered.

A mapmaker from Germany read about Vespucci's voyage and was fascinated. He created a map of the new land. He called the new land "America" after Vespucci's first name, Amerigo. The name caught on and people everywhere called the New World "America."

Answer the questions on the next page.

Practice determining the author's purpose by answering questions about the article you just read. Read each question. Circle the letter of the best answer.

1. What is this passage mostly about?

   A how America got its name

   B Columbus sailing to America

   C how America was explored

   D Amerigo Vespucci's voyage

2. The middle paragraphs of this passage provide —

   A the author's opinion about exploring

   B general information about explorers

   C facts about some explorers

   D entertaining stories about exploration

3. Which fact from the story helps provide the author's purpose?

   A He called the new land "America" after Vespucci's first name, Amerigo.

   B We even celebrate Columbus Day in his honor.

   C Christopher Columbus was the first European explorer to reach America.

   D Vespucci was from Italy, just like Columbus.

4. This passage is best described as —

   A a funny story

   B a convincing opinion

   C an informative article

   D a journal entry

5. The author's purpose is probably to —

   A give you information

   B persuade you

   C describe something to you

   D entertain you

6. Find one sentence from the passage that is written in a persuasive way. On a separate sheet of paper, explain how you know it is persuasive.

DINOSAUR VOMIT DISCOVERED

Scientists are learning about dinosaurs from their vomit.

PETERBOROUGH, ENGLAND—It appears that even dinosaurs sometimes had trouble holding down their food! Scientists recently uncovered the remains of a dinosaur's vomit in a Peterborough, England, **quarry.** The vomit fossil is about 160 million years old.

While such a discovery might make some people sick to their stomachs, scientists are "throwing up" their arms in delight. "We believe that this is the first time the existence of fossil vomit on a grand scale has been proven beyond reasonable doubt," said geologist Peter Doyle.

Studies revealed that the prehistoric vomit may have belonged to an ichthyosaur, a large, sea-dwelling dinosaur. The vomit contained dozens of ancient squid-like shellfish, which was one of the ichthyosaur's favorite foods. Scientists believe the tough shells may have given the dinosaur indigestion.

The ill ichthyosaur may have eaten the shellfish whole, then vomited the hard-to-stomach shells. This sloppy style of eating is still done by sperm whales and other animals today. It looks like some creatures never learn!

Doyle and his research team presented the unique dino discovery at a conference at the University of Copenhagen, Denmark.

Write About It

One of the author's purposes in writing this article is to inform. Another purpose is to entertain. On a separate sheet of paper, list several words, phrases, or sentences the author uses to inform and to entertain.

Read this article about UFOs. Then answer the questions on the next page.

Lights in the Sky

While scientists have made many discoveries, there is even more that they do not know. Old ideas are constantly being questioned. Each day, for example, people are discovering new stars and planets. It is certainly possible that there are living creatures in space—they may even be watching us from above.

Over the years, hundreds of people have looked up at the sky and seen unidentified flying objects, or UFOs. Many UFOs turn out to be natural or man-made objects, such as clouds or weather balloons. Some sightings, however, have never been explained. These Unidentified Flying Objects could be spaceships from another world.

Many people have reported seeing silver, disk-shaped objects flying through the daytime sky. Often, the disks fly at impossible speeds, or they **hover** without moving or making noise. Surely, these objects are not airplanes, weather balloons, or some other familiar object. Some of these flying disks were photographed by onlookers. Some of the objects in the photos have been identified, but others seem to be genuine mysteries. Someday, we may be able to prove that the unfamiliar objects really are from another planet.

Besides objects, people have also seen unexplainable lights in the night sky. These lights seem to hover, change colors, or move at incredible speeds. It has been proven that they are not meteors, comets, or satellites. There is no explanation for them. They have also been photographed and even videotaped. It is hard to believe that the lights are not from an alien spacecraft.

Most people who report seeing UFOs are intelligent, believable people. They would probably know if they had seen something as common as an airplane or a weather balloon. It may just be that they have caught a glimpse of visitors from another planet. Wouldn't it be interesting if those visitors had pictures of us, too!

Read each question. Circle the letter of the best answer.

1. What is the first paragraph mostly about?

    A We are discovering new planets in the sky.

    B There are many things science can't explain.

    C Scientists don't believe in UFOs.

    D Science is wrong.

2. In the fourth paragraph, the phrase *It is hard to believe* signals that the author is telling —

    A a fact

    B an opinion

    C an explanation

    D a story

3. The author gives the ideas in the fourth paragraph in order to —

    A describe the lights in the sky

    B prove that UFOs exist

    C entertain the reader with UFO stories

    D show that some unidentified lights might be from alien ships

4. One word in the final paragraph that shows that the author might be giving an opinion is —

    A believable

    B history

    C planet

    D visitors

5. The facts and ideas in this article —

    A seem to point to one conclusion

    B describe a UFO

    C make an entertaining story

    D are definitely true

6. The author's opinion seems to be that —

    A UFOs could not be aliens

    B UFOs are definitely aliens

    C there are no such things as UFOs

    D UFOs might be aliens

7. What is the author's purpose in writing this article?

    A to give facts about UFOs

    B to convince you that UFOs could be aliens

    C to convince you that UFOs are definitely aliens

    D to entertain you

8. Find one sentence from the passage that is written to inform. Write it on a separate sheet of paper.

Before you begin this lesson, take this quiz to show what you know about problems and solutions. First, read this story about a daring escape. Then answer the questions that follow.

Fire Escape

The forest fire roared higher, creeping closer and closer to the cliff where Manuel stood. He looked over the edge. It must have been a hundred feet down. The only way across was the tiny cable bridge. Danielle stood on the other side.

"Come on!" she screamed. "You've got to get across the river! There's no time."

Manuel looked behind him. The blazing fire and choking smoke were coming closer. He looked at the bridge. It looked so thin and weak. The river was a long way down. Looking down, Manuel got dizzy.

"Don't look down!" Danielle shouted over the roar of the flames. "Just look at me. Imagine you're walking on the sidewalk."

Manuel gulped. He could feel the heat of the fire as it surrounded him from behind. He stepped out onto the narrow plank of the bridge. He watched Danielle. He imagined he was walking on a sidewalk. Manuel was able to breathe easier. He put one foot in front of the other, holding tight to the railing. Finally, he stepped onto solid ground on the other side.

Circle the letter of the best answer.

1. What is dangerous about this situation?

    A Danielle is mean.

    B The fire is coming closer.

    C Manuel is near the forest.

    D There is no bridge.

2. What is a reason Manuel doesn't want to cross the bridge?

    A He dislikes the other side.

    B The bridge is broken.

    C He is afraid of heights.

    D He doesn't like Danielle.

3. How does Danielle help Manuel?

    A She crosses the bridge.

    B She puts out the fire.

    C She tells Manuel to look at her.

    D She stands on the other side.

4. How was Manuel able to breathe easier?

    A by looking down at the river

    B by crossing the bridge

    C by imagining he was on a sidewalk

    D by gulping

Introduction

Many stories and articles have **problems and solutions**. A **problem** is something that causes trouble or is difficult. A **solution** is how to solve the problem.

To identify problems and solutions,

- Look for the trouble the characters face or have.
- Think about why this trouble is a problem.
- Look for the event or step that solves the problem. How does the character solve the problem?

Here's How

Read these sentences. How might Mrs. Croft's problem be solved?

Mrs. Croft watched the clock. The computers had been dead for five minutes, and she needed to know what to do. Suddenly the principal walked in, and she breathed easier. He would take care of things.

Think About It

1. The trouble is that the computers are dead.

2. The computers being dead is a problem because Mrs. Croft probably needs them for her class.

3. The principal's arrival is the solution because "he will take care of things."

Try This Strategy

Predict

When you **predict,** you look over the passage before reading and guess what it might be about.

- Look at the title and pictures and read the first sentence. Try to guess what the passage will be about.
- As you read, think about whether your predictions were correct.
- Make new predictions as you find out more.

Read the story. Use the Reading Guide for tips. The tips will help you predict and identify problems and solutions as you read.

Reading Guide

Look at the title and picture. Try to predict what problem the characters in the story might face.

Think about the problem with the computers. Imagine how it might be solved.

Think about the characters. Predict who is most likely to solve the problem.

THE COMPUTER WIZARD

Mrs. Croft watched the clock. The computers had been dead for five minutes, and she needed to know what to do. Suddenly the principal walked in, and she breathed easier. He would take care of things.

"It's not just this room. The whole school is down," he said gravely. "Our tech guy doesn't know what went wrong."

The principal surveyed the room, hoping for an answer. Slouched in the corner was Wizard Williams.

"Wizard?" he said. Everyone called him that because he was a computer whiz.

"I'm on it," Wizard said. He followed the vice principal down the stairs and through a dark hallway. In a back room, a thin man with glasses was shaking his head. In front of him was the blank screen of the school's main computer.

"Let me handle this," Wizard said, sitting down. With a few keystrokes, the screen came back to life. From far above, he heard cheers coming from above. The wizard had worked his magic again.

Now use what you learned to identify problems and solutions.

Answer the questions on the next page.

Practice identifying problems and solutions in the story you just read.

EXAMPLE

What does the principal do that helps him find a solution?

A He talks to the tech guy.

B He finds Wizard Williams.

C He comes into the room.

D He fixes the computer.

Look for what is causing trouble for the characters.

The computers are dead, and the tech guy doesn't know what went wrong.

Think about why this causes a problem.

This is a problem because the students need the computers for class, and he doesn't know who will fix them.

Look for the event or step that solves the problem.

Seeing Wizard helps the principal find the solution of having Wizard fix the computers.

Now read each question. Circle the letter of the best answer.

1. What is the main problem in the story?

   A Wizard needs to save the day.

   B The computers crashed.

   C The tech guy is shaking his head.

   D Mrs. Croft watches the clock.

2. What trouble has this problem caused?

   A The tech guy is shaking his head.

   B The clock stopped.

   C The students cannot do their computer work.

   D The students cheer.

3. What is the solution to the main problem in the story?

   A The tech guy fixes the computers.

   B The computers go dead.

   C The principal enters the room.

   D Wizard fixes the computers.

4. What action solves the main problem?

   A Cheers come from the classroom.

   B Wizard makes a few keystrokes on the computer.

   C Wizard is slouched in the corner.

   D Wizard and the principal walk down the hall.

NEWS FLASH!

Mayor Violates Snowball Law

Throwing snowballs was illegal in Topeka.

TOPEKA, KS—The mayor of Topeka turned himself in after an Illinois girl showed that he had **violated** the law. His crime? Throwing a snowball at a tree.

Kristen Aberle of Thawville, Illinois, wrote a letter to Mayor Bill Bunten when she learned about a law against throwing snowballs. She learned about it and other "dumb laws" in her government class.

When the mayor received the letter, he first thought it was a joke. When he realized that he had violated the law, he turned himself in to the police. Then he began working to overturn the law, "lest our already-crowded prisons are filled up with children."

Under the original law, people can be fined up to $499 and spend 179 days in jail for throwing a snowball, stone, or other object. Bunten asked the city attorney to write a new law that leaves out the part about snowballs.

✏ Write About It

Now practice the skill using a real news story. Fill in the graphic organizer to show what problem Mayor Bunten had and how he solved it.

Problem	Solution

Review

You have learned that a **problem** is something that causes trouble or difficulty. The **solution** is an action that solves the problem.

Review the steps that help identify problems and solutions.

- Look for the things that cause trouble in the passage.
- List the events, steps, or ideas in the passage.
- Identify the event, step, or idea that helps solve the problem.

Practice 1

Read the following passage. As you read, find the problem that the crows have. How do they solve the problem?

> Crows are amazingly intelligent. In Japan, several crows had a problem. They had a hard time cracking open some tough nuts. The crows carried the nuts to a street corner. They waited for the "walk" sign. Then they placed the nuts in the crosswalk and went back to the corner. When the lights changed, cars drove over the nuts. Their tires cracked the shells open. When the "walk" sign flashed again, the crows grabbed the cracked nuts!

List the problem in the first box and the solution in the second.

Problem	Solution

Practice 2

Read the passage. How does the girl solve her problem?

Sarah had reached the end of the street fair when she realized her **bandanna** was gone. She had worn that bandanna when she scored the goal in the championship game last year. Sarah looked back into the crowd. Thousands of people crowded the street. She must have visited fifty booths.

"I'll never find it. Someone probably took it by now," Sarah wailed.

Carlos, her older brother, put his hand on her shoulder. "Where did you take it off?" he asked.

"I don't remember," Sarah cried.

"Think back. Did you put anything else on your head?" he asked. Sarah had tried on a skull mask at the booth for Dia de los Muertos, or Day of the Dead. She and Carlos dashed back to the booth. There, next to the skeletons and ornaments, was her championship bandanna.

Use this graphic organizer to identify problem and solution.

Problem	
Solution	

Practice 3

Read the passage. Then identify problems and solutions to answer the questions. Make a graphic organizer on a separate sheet of paper to organize your thoughts.

> Trisha made friendship bracelets and sold them at school. Each week, she would count her money, and then count back the amount she had paid for thread. She had saved up almost enough money to buy a video game system.
>
> "No video games until your math grades get better," Mom said. Trisha almost cried. She hated math. She couldn't work out the numbers on paper. She would forget to carry a one, or she would mix up the steps.
>
> Trisha had a big test on Wednesday. That morning, she sold twelve more bracelets. She put her money in her pocket.
>
> *Why is it that I can count money so well, but I can't do math?* she thought. Just then, she had an idea. She could use the money to help her.
>
> In math class, Trisha laid her money on her desk. The first problem on the math test was decimals. She counted out bills for the whole numbers. Then, she used change for the decimal numbers. Trisha realized that subtracting decimals was as easy as counting backward. Trisha's teacher looked over Trisha's shoulder. But once she saw that Trisha was doing her own work, she smiled.
>
> The next day, Trisha got back her math test. She'd gotten a 94! And with those last twelve bracelets, she could finally get her video game system.

1. What is Trisha's problem?

_____

_____

2. What makes Trisha's problem especially bad for her?

_____

_____

3. How does Trisha solve her problem?

_____

_____

Introduction

Problems and solutions often form the main action or idea of a story or article. A **problem** is something that causes trouble. The **solution** is how the problem is fixed.

As you saw on pages 139–141, graphic organizers can help you identify problems and solutions.

- In the first box, describe the problem.
- In the second box, explain why this is a problem.
- In the third box, write the action or event that solves the problem.

Here's How

Read these sentences. How does Austin solve his problem?

Austin Meggitt of Amherst, Ohio, was having a hard time carrying his bat and glove on his bicycle to baseball practice. So he invented a special carrying **caddy.**

Think About It

Trouble	Why This Is a Problem	Action That Solves Problem
Austin has trouble carrying his bat and glove on his bicycle.	He needed his bat and glove for practice.	He invented a caddy that helps him carry his stuff.

Try This Strategy

Monitor and Clarify

When you **monitor and clarify,** you check to make sure you understand what you are reading. If you do not understand, use skills and strategies to help you.

- At the end of each paragraph, stop reading and try to recall what the paragraph was about.
- If you do not understand the paragraph, reread it or ask yourself questions about it.
- Look for changes in the focus of the passage.

Read the article. Use the Reading Guide for tips that can help you monitor and clarify and identify problem and solution as you read.

Reading Guide

Clarify what the first paragraph is about. What problem did KK have? How was it solved?

How does the focus of the article change in the third paragraph?

Watch for the problem each person faces. Can you see how each problem is solved?

Kid Inventors

Ten-year-old KK Gregory was building a snow fort. Her wrists started to get red and raw. There was a gap between her mittens and her coat, and snow was making her wrists cold. So what did she do? KK invented Wristies, a wrist protector that kept her wrists warm. She is now selling Wristies on TV and across the country.

Kids can be inventors, too. Usually, people think of an invention when they have a problem. The invention is a new way to solve that problem. Sometimes, kids look at a problem in a new way that adults don't see.

Krysta Morlan had an itchy, sore cast. She invented a cast cooler that pumped air over her skin. Ten-year-old Johnny Bodylski noticed that some people left their sprinklers on even when it was raining. This wasted water, so he built a sprinkler that had a rain **sensor** on it. The sensor turned off the sprinkler when it rained, and turned it back on when the ground got dry. Austin Meggitt of Amherst, Ohio, was having a hard time carrying his bat and glove on his bicycle to baseball practice. He invented a special carrying **caddy.**

Look around. Do you see something in your life that is hard to do, or isn't working right? Invent a solution!

Answer the questions on the next page.

Practice identifying problems and solutions by answering questions about the article you just read. Read each question. Circle the letter of the best answer.

1. What was giving KK Gregory trouble?

   A Her wrists got cold.

   B She saw the problem in a new way.

   C She had no mittens.

   D Her cast itched.

2. What caused KK's problem?

   A The weather was too cold for playing outside.

   B She was only a kid.

   C There was a gap between her mittens and coat.

   D She was wasting water.

3. Krysta Morlan decided to create a new invention because —

   A her wrists were cold

   B she had an itchy cast

   C her sprinkler was wasting water

   D she couldn't carry her equipment on her bike

4. How did Johnny Bodylski solve his problem?

   A He turned off his sprinkler.

   B He put a rain sensor on the sprinkler.

   C He stopped watering the lawn.

   D He told people they were wasting water.

5. What helped to solve each problem in this story?

   A giving up

   B a trip to the store

   C asking an adult

   D a new invention

6. On a separate sheet of paper, describe a problem you have seen. Think of an invention that could solve that problem.

A parakeet nest caused a blackout in Edgewater, New Jersey.

PARAKEETS CAUSE BLACKOUT, 150 LOSE POWER

EDGEWATER, NJ—A parakeet nest caused a fire and a blackout that left 150 homes without power in Edgewater, New Jersey. The exotic monk parakeets had built a six-foot-tall nest on top of an electrical pole.

A spark from a power line lit the twigs in the nest. The small blaze shut down a **transformer,** cutting off electricity. Firefighters put out the fire shortly after the alarm sounded.

The monk parakeets are native to South America, but have been nesting in the town of Edgewater for over a decade. Researchers believe they began as pets that escaped or were let go. Large colonies have also been found in Miami, Dallas, and other cities. The tropical birds commonly nest near transformers because the devices provide warmth.

The power outage has angered some residents, who say the birds are pests and should be removed. Monk parakeets have also been blamed for destroying garden plants and annoying residents with loud shrieking. Other Edgewater residents insist the parakeets have a right to stay, saying that they add life and natural beauty to the city.

The power company plans to remove the nests from the power lines to solve the parakeet problem.

Write About It

Read this sentence from the article: "The power company plans to remove the nests from the power lines to solve the parakeet problem." It presents a solution to a problem. On a separate sheet of paper, describe the parakeet problem using information from the article.

Read this passage about demolition. Then answer the questions on the next page.

IMPLOSION!

An old apartment building stands vacant. It will be torn down to make room for a new recreation center. But it might take weeks to tear down the building with cranes, wrecking balls, and bulldozers. How can the building be destroyed more quickly? And how can it be done without damaging the neighborhood around it?

The answer is **implosion.** Implosion is like explosion, but the force goes in or down instead of up and out. People who implode buildings work in a special industry called **demolition.** Imploding a building takes a lot more than just putting some explosives in the basement. Implosion is a carefully controlled process that requires training, skill, and perfect timing.

If a building is to be imploded, it must be prepared. Everything in the building is taken out—the furniture, the computers, and the appliances. Next, much of the inside structure of the building is removed. The demolition workers take out many of the inside walls. They remove any glass that could fly out and cut someone.

Next, the demolition crew looks carefully at how the building is made. They locate the beams and supports that hold the building up. They carefully place a few explosives around these beams and supports. The crew tries to use as few explosives as possible. The idea is to make the building fall in on itself, not blow up.

All of the explosives are put on timers. These timers make sure that each support is destroyed so that the building falls straight down, instead of sideways onto other buildings.

The last step is to clear the area around the building. The streets and buildings around the implosion are off-limits to anyone. An implosion is an amazing sight to see, and many people want to get a close look. The demolition company must be very careful that spectators are kept a safe distance away.

When everything is set, the demolition crew flips the switch. The building is destroyed quickly and safely, making room for new structures.

Read each question. Circle the letter of the best answer.

1. Why can't the apartment building remain standing?

   A It has ceased to be fit for business or residence.

   B It is ugly.

   C It has to make room for a new recreation center.

   D It is worn out.

2. Workers cannot use bulldozers or wrecking balls because —

   A they are too expensive

   B they are too slow

   C they aren't exciting

   D they are too difficult to use

3. How might the destruction of one building cause trouble for the others in the neighborhood?

   A The recreation center will be ugly.

   B It will attract spectators.

   C It could damage other buildings.

   D There will be many workers around.

4. How could glass cause trouble?

   A It is too heavy.

   B It is too expensive to destroy.

   C It is difficult to break.

   D It could fly out and cut someone.

5. What is the quickest way to destroy the building?

   A implosion

   B with a crane

   C with a wrecking ball

   D with bulldozers

6. How do the demolition workers make sure that the building falls straight down?

   A They pull on it with cranes.

   B They take out all the furniture.

   C They put explosives in the basement.

   D They put the explosives on timers.

7. Spectators must be kept a safe distance away because they —

   A don't know how to time the explosives

   B want to save the building

   C must be safe

   D might flip the switch

8. On a separate sheet of paper, list all the problems that an implosion might help solve.

148

Glossary

absorption the ability to soak up (Lesson 2)

abundant available in great quantity (Lesson 8)

access prior knowledge to think about something you already know and use it to understand what you read (Lesson 2, Lesson 7, Lesson 8)

amphitheater an oval building that is used as a stadium or theater (Lesson 9)

aquarium a glass tank in which living animals or plants are kept (Lesson 6)

architecture the designing of buildings (Lesson 7)

author's purpose the reason that an author writes a story (Lesson 9)

bacteria tiny living cells that can only be seen with a microscope (Lesson 3)

bamboo a tall plant with a narrow stem, often found in warm areas (Lesson 1)

bandanna a square piece of cloth worn around the neck or head (Lesson 10)

caddy a carrying case for a collection of items (Lesson 10)

cause and effect a cause is an event that makes something happen; the effect is what happens (Lesson 3)

chlorine a chemical used to kill germs (Lesson 3)

coincidence a series of events which appear related but actually happen by chance (Lesson 2)

commotion a noisy confusion (Lesson 3)

compare and contrast to find ways things are alike and different (Lesson 1)

complex a group of related parts (Lesson 9)

context clues words or phrases that help with the understanding of a new word (Lesson 4)

cougar a large, powerful, brownish-yellow wild American cat (Lesson 6)

daring willing to take risks; brave (Lesson 4)

demolition knocking down; destroying (Lesson 10)

descend to move downward (Lesson 7)

detect to notice; to discover (Lesson 1)

dispatcher a person who quickly sends a message, usually over a radio (Lesson 6)

distributed spread out (Lesson 2)

draw conclusions to make reasonable judgments based on details you read (Lesson 6)

dwindle to become less; to shrink slowly (Lesson 5)

easel a stand or rack used to hold a painting (Lesson 5)

elaborate made with great detail (Lesson 3)

enlist to get help from someone (Lesson 2)

enormous extremely large; huge (Lesson 6)

expedition a trip made by a group of people for a specific purpose (Lesson 8)

extraordinary very unusual or remarkable (Lesson 6)

fact and opinion a fact is a statement that can be proved true or false; an opinion is a statement that tells how someone thinks or feels (Lesson 8)

fatality a death (Lesson 5)

figurative language words that create an image in a reader's head (Lesson 7)

freestyle a contest in which competitors choose their own style and moves (Lesson 8)

hilarious very funny (Lesson 1)

hornbook a printed page attached to a wood paddle and covered by a clear material (Lesson 1)

hover to float in the air without moving (Lesson 9)

hunch a guess about what will happen (Lesson 9)

implosion a bursting inward (Lesson 10)

initiate to cause something to begin (Lesson 9)

innovator someone who does something differently than it has been done before (Lesson 8)

invasion the act of armed forces moving into another country in order to take it over (Lesson 6)

knucklebone a rounded bone found in a knuckle (Lesson 1)

laborer a person whose job requires that they work with their hands (Lesson 3)

linger to stay longer than necessary (Lesson 9)

listless without interest or energy (Lesson 7)

main idea and details the most important idea or event of a passage or paragraph and the facts or events that support it (Lesson 5)

malfunction to work incorrectly (Lesson 2)

manually by hand (Lesson 2)

metallic having the quality of metal (Lesson 8)

monitor and clarify to make sure that you understand what you are reading (Lesson 3, Lesson 5, Lesson 7, Lesson 10)

myth a story that is not true but has been told for a long time (Lesson 9)

nuisance something that is annoying or bothersome (Lesson 6)

particle a tiny object that cannot be seen (Lesson 5)

pester annoy; bother (Lesson 6)

physical to do with the body (Lesson 4)

precaution care taken beforehand to prevent harm (Lesson 6)

predict to look for clues about a passage and make a guess about what you will read (Lesson 5, Lesson 6, Lesson 9, Lesson 10)

problems and solutions a problem is something that causes trouble or difficulty; a solution is a way to solve a problem by making it go away or finding a way around it (Lesson 10)

quarry a place where stone is dug from the ground (Lesson 9)

radiation energy that is given off by something (Lesson 5)

realistic showing people, things, and events as they are in everyday life (Lesson 1)

reputation a commonly held belief about a person or group (Lesson 3)

rodent a small animal, such as a squirrel or rat, with sharp front teeth used to chew (Lesson 1)

scan and skim to look through a passage quickly to get an idea of what it is about or to find a particular part (Lesson 1, Lesson 4, Lesson 8)

scarce uncommon; difficult to find (Lesson 5)

sensor a device that detects the presence of something (Lesson 10)

sequence the order in which things happen (Lesson 2)

sewer a pipe under the ground that carries waste from sinks and toilets (Lesson 3)

shriek to make a loud, high-pitched sound (Lesson 4)

somnambulism the act of sleepwalking (Lesson 4)

summarize to retell the most important parts of a story or passage in your own words (Lesson 2, Lesson 9)

superstitious believing that certain actions have magical powers (Lesson 2)

taffy a chewy candy made with sugar and butter (Lesson 9)

transaction an exchange of money or goods (Lesson 8)

transformer a device that changes the power of electricity (Lesson 10)

transmitter a machine that sends a radio signal (Lesson 7)

turnstile a gate that turns to allow one person to enter at a time (Lesson 2)

uncharted not mapped or thoroughly explored (Lesson 8)

violate to go against; to break (Lesson 10)

virtually nearly; almost entirely (Lesson 6)

visualize to picture in your mind what you are reading (Lesson 1, Lesson 3, Lesson 6)

whimper to cry weakly (Lesson 5)

Notes

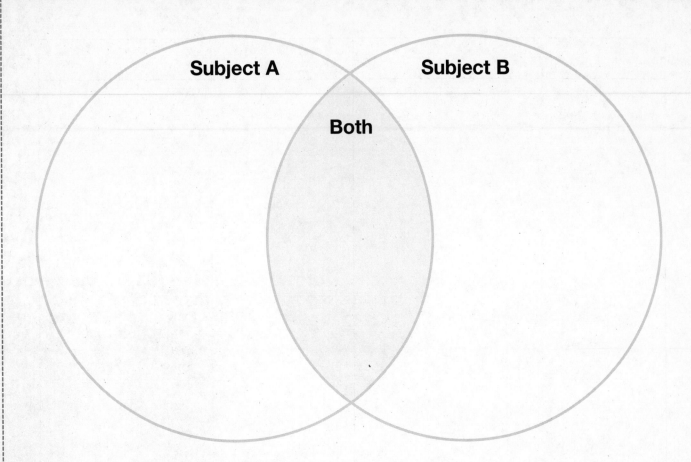

Subject A **Subject B**

Both

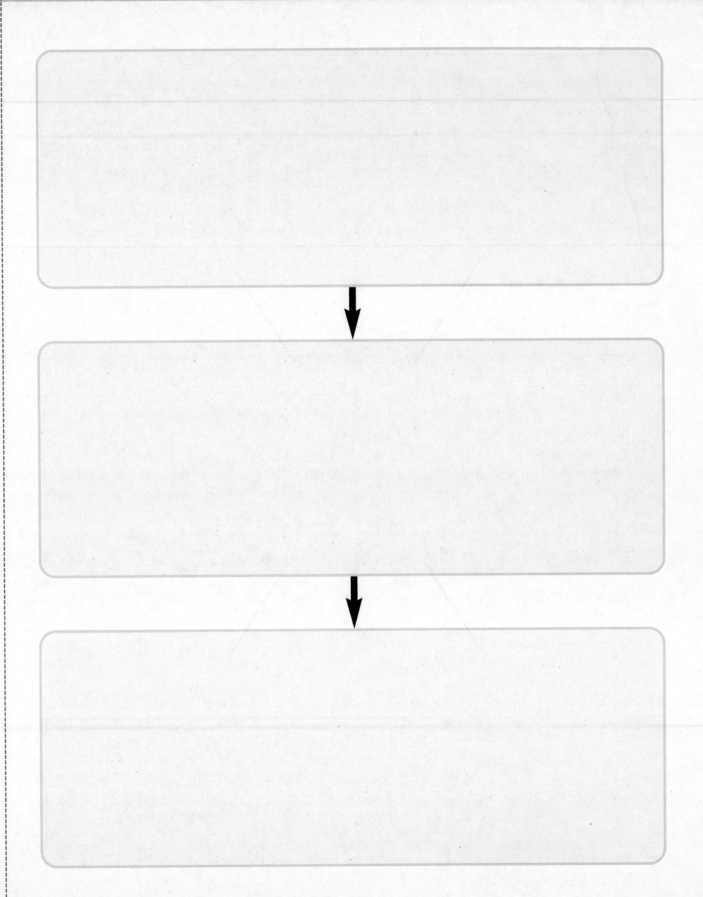

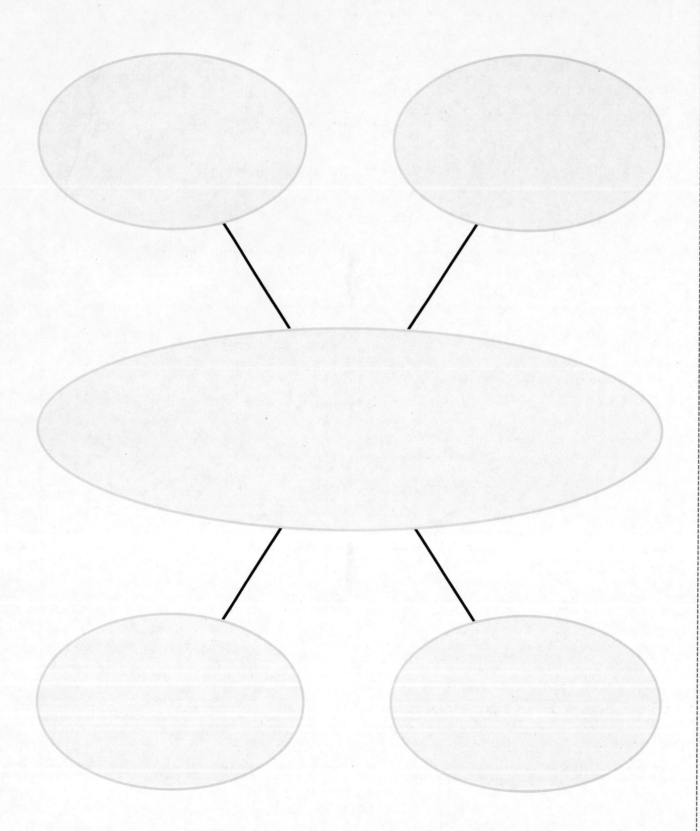

1.

2.

3.

4.

5.

6.

7.

8.

9.

10.

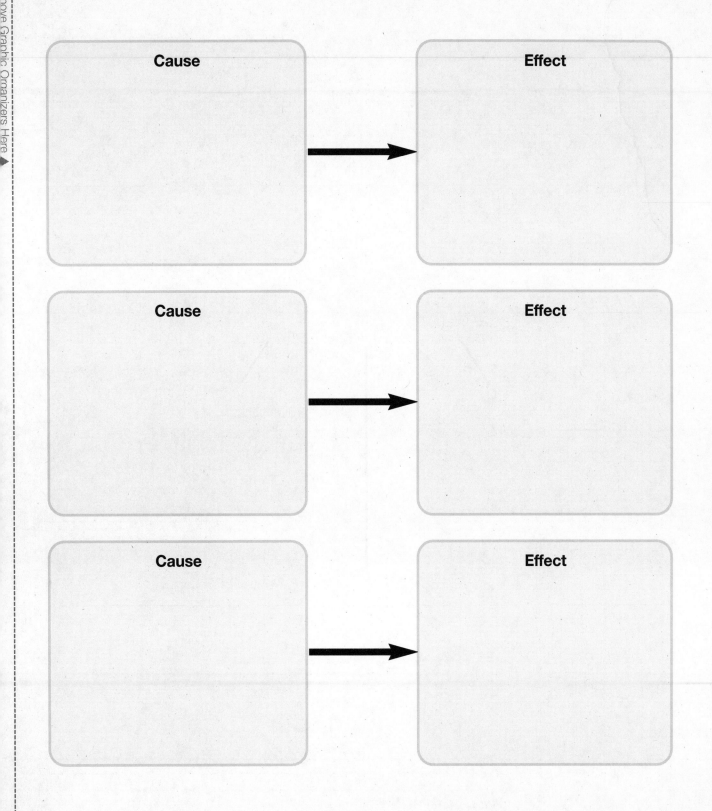

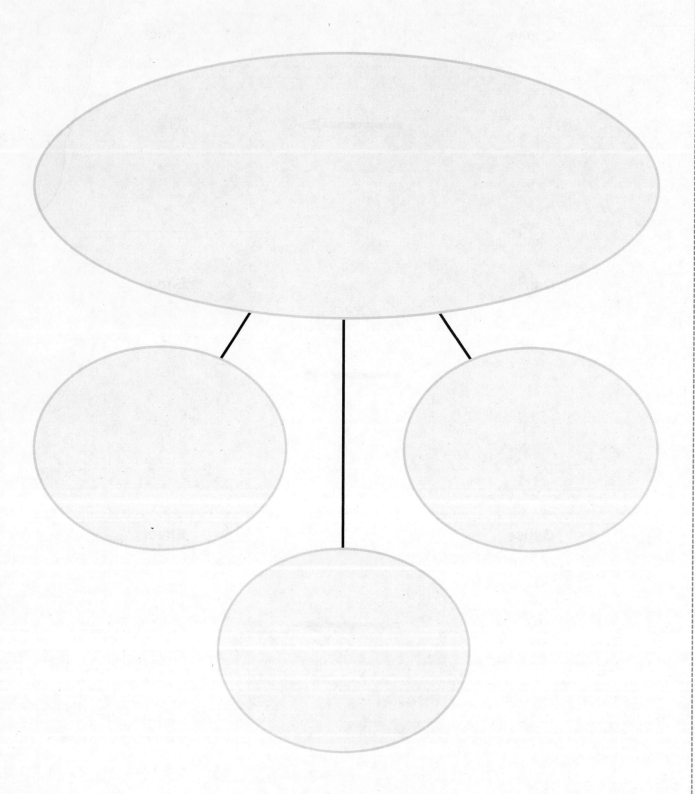